**Job Interview Questions Series**

# BASE SAS
## INTERVIEW QUESTIONS
## YOU'LL MOST LIKELY BE ASKED

**291**
Interview Questions

**VIBRANT**
P U B L I S H E R S

# Base SAS

## Interview Questions
## You'll Most Likely Be Asked

ISBN-10: 1-946383-78-3
ISBN-13: 978-1-946383-78-5

Library of Congress Control Number: 2012906684

This publication is designed to provide accurate and authoritative information in regard to the subject matter covered. The author has made every effort in the preparation of this book to ensure the accuracy of the information. However, information in this book is sold without warranty either expressed or implied. The Author or the Publisher will not be liable for any damages caused or alleged to be caused either directly or indirectly by this book.

Vibrant Publishers books are available at special quantity discount for sales promotions, or for use in corporate training programs. For more information please write to **bulkorders@vibrantpublishers.com**

Please email feedback / corrections (technical, grammatical or spelling) to **spellerrors@vibrantpublishers.com**

To access the complete catalogue of Vibrant Publishers, visit **www.vibrantpublishers.com**

# Table of Contents

Dear Reader,

Thank you for purchasing **Base SAS Interview Questions You'll Most Likely Be Asked**. We are committed to publishing books that are content-rich, concise and approachable enabling more readers to read and make the fullest use of them. We hope this book provides the most enriching learning experience as you prepare for your interview.

Should you have any questions or suggestions, feel free to email us at **reachus@vibrantpublishers.com**

Thanks again for your purchase. Good luck with your interview!

- Vibrant Publishers Team

# **Base** SAS
# Interview Questions

Review these typical interview questions and think about how you would answer them. Read the answers listed; you will find best possible answers along with strategies and suggestions.

This page is intentionally left blank

# Chapter 1

# Basics

---

**1: Explain SAS and its functions.**

**Answer:**

SAS is a popular Statistical Analysis System used for data analytics. It contains a set of software tools that are well integrated to extract, compile and process the data including Big Data. SAS performs the following functions:

a) Data Warehousing

b) Statistical scrutiny of the information, data mining and metrics

c) Helps the businesses in planning and forecasting

d) Provides statistical data for decision-making

e) Retrieving and managing useful business information

f) Presenting the available information as reports and

graphics

g) Process research and Project management

h) Improving Quality by providing valuable insights

i) Application Development

**2: What are the different types of output produced by SAS?**

**Answer:**

A SAS program can typically produce one or more of the following outputs:

a) **A SAS Data Set** – a temporary or permanent table that contains the observations and variables.

b) **A Report or Listing** – a list of information or a DATA SET or a summary report containing the information/statistics.

c) **SAS Log** – a log file that contains the list of statements used and the corresponding results or messages from SAS. The log can also be a display on screen or printout.

d) **Catalogue** – Graphs and other output produced by the SAS program which cannot be stored as a Data Set can be included in the catalogue.

e) **External file or database** – such as Oracle or MS Access which can be accessed and modified by SAS programs.

f) **ODS Output** – Apart from these, the SAS Output Delivery System can produce outputs in HTML, PostScript, and RTF formats in addition to SAS listings and Data Sets.

**3: You might be already familiar with the Data Set. What is the descriptor portion of the Data Set?**

**Answer:**

Descriptor portion of the Data Set contains information about the Data Set like name of the Data Set, date and time when it was created, number of observation, number of variables and attribute information for each variable in the Data Set.

### 4: Which parameters describe a variable in SAS?

**Answer:**

A variable can be best described by its Length, Type, Name, Label, FORMAT and INFORMAT in SAS.

### 5: How does SAS recognise the end of a step and execute the previous step?

**Answer:**

Whenever SAS encounters a DATA, PROC, RUN or QUIT statement, SAS executes the previous step.

### 6: How can a permanent SAS Data Set be referenced?

**Answer:**

A permanent SAS Data Set can be referenced by a 2-level name: *'libref.filename'*. LIBREF is library name to which SAS file belongs and FILENAME is the Data Set name. LIBREF and FILENAME are separated by a period.

*Example:* To reference a SAS Data Set named *questionset1* (stored in the library *exam)*, we use the two-level name -*exam.questionset1*.

### 7: What is the default length of numeric variables?

**Answer:**

Numeric variables are stored as floating-point numbers in 8 bytes of storage unless we specify different length. The default length of numeric variables is 8.

# Chapter 2

# Referencing Files

**8: How do you refer an external file in SAS?**

**Answer:**

External files can be accessed in SAS programs in 3 ways – using the FILE, INFILE or %INCLUDE statements. The FILE statement gives you direct access to the lines input using the PUT statement. It requires the FILENAME and LIBNAME specified in the variables of FILENAME and LIBNAME types to access the file. The INFILE statement lets you direct access to the file without using any other object or variable type. With INFILE, you can directly access the file by specifying its path along with the INFILE statement. Otherwise, it functions like the FILE statement. While the FILE and INFILE statements give you access to each line of its content, the %INCLUDE statement loads the entire file into the SAS engine.

## 9: Explain the GSUBMIT Command.

**Answer:**

The GSUBMIT command is used to submit or commit the SAS statements in the windows buffer permanently. It can also be used to submit or commit the SAS statements in the current program. The SAS statements in the windows buffer will not be committed using the GSUBMIT while the program is still running.

## 10: How do you verify after assigning a LIBREF?

**Answer:**

When a LIBNAME statement is submitted, a message is displayed in log window stating that LIBREF has been successfully assigned. Thus, checking the log window enables us to verify the LIBREF.

## 11: What is the purpose of a SAS engine?

**Answer:**

SAS engine is the set of internal instructions which SAS uses for writing to and reading from files in the SAS library.SAS can read or write files by using appropriate engine for that file type.

## 12: Describe some ways to view the contents of SAS Data Set.

**Answer:**

There are three ways for viewing the contents of a SAS Data Set-PROCCONTENTS, PROC Data Sets and opening the *libraries* folder in the explored window.

*Example:* To view the contents of a Data Set *'questionset2'* stored in the library *'exam'* the following programs can be used.

*proc contents data=exam.questionset2;*

*run;*

OR

*proc datasets;*

*contents data=exam.questionset2;*

*quit;*

**13: Which option is used to list the variables in creation order or order of logical position while viewing the Data Set with PROC CONTENTS?**

**Answer:**

VARNUM OPTION can be used for listing the variables in logical order. By default, PROC CONTENTS and PROC Data Sets list variables alphabetically. Specifying VARNUM option causes the variables to be listed in the order of logical position.

The following example illustrates the use of VARNUM option with PROC CONTENTS.VARNUM option causes the variables in the Data Set *questionset2* to be listed in the creation order.

*proc contents data=exam.questionset2 varnum;*

*run;*

**14: How do you modify SAS system options like page number, time etc?**

**Answer:**

OPTIONS STATEMENT can be submitted to modify system options.

In the following example an OPTIONS statement is submitted to change the following options- *date* and PAGENO. Since the option is set to NODATE, SAS displays no date in the output. Also, in the output, the numbering of the page starts from 3 since PAGENO option is set to 3.

*options nodate pageno=3;*

*proc contents data=exam.questionset2 varnum;*

*run;*


### 15: How does SAS handles two-digit year values?

**Answer:**

When SAS reads two-digit year values it is interpreted based on 100-year span which starts with YEARCUTOFF=value. The default value of YEARCUTOFF= is *1920*.

It is possible to override the default value and change the value of YEARCUTOFF= to the first year of another 100-year span.


### 16: Suppose your Data Set *exam.questionset2* contains 20 observations. How do you print only the last 11 observations?

**Answer:**

This can be achieved by using FIRSTOBS=10 option. SAS reads tenth observation first and then reads till the last observation.

*Example:*

*options firstobs=10;*

*proc print data=exam.questionset2;*

   *run;*


### 17: Suppose your Data Set *exam.questionset2* contains 20 observations. How do you print the observations from 12-17?

**Answer:**

This can be achieved by combining FIRSTOBS= and OBS= option.

*Example:*

*options firstobs=12 obs=17;*

*proc print data=exam.questionset2;*

*run;*

**18: Describe the SOURCE system option used in SAS.**

**Answer:**

The SOURCE system option controls whether SAS source statements are to be written to SAS log. The default system setting is SOURCE.

The syntax is SOURCE | NOSOURCE.

**SOURCE** - specifies to write SAS SOURCE statements to SAS log.

**NOSOURCE** - specifies not to write SAS SOURCE statements to SAS log.

**19: Describe the REPLACE option in detail.**

**Answer:**

This specifies that the permanently stored Data Sets can be replaced. If the option NOREPLACE is used the inadvertent replacing of existing Data Sets can be prevented.

The syntax is REPLACE | NOREPLACE.

**REPLACE** - specifies that a permanently stored Data Set can be replaced with another Data Set of same name.

**NOREPLACE** - specifies that a permanently stored Data Set cannot be replaced with another Data Set of same name. This helps in preventing replacing Data Sets by mistake.

This page is intentionally left blank

# Chapter 3

# SAS Programs

**20: What is the purpose of adding @@ in an input statement after the variable?**

**Answer:**

Usually, to input each record in SAS, you need a separate input statement. With @@ at the end of an input statement, SAS will wait to continue with the input statement. So, if you have multiple records to input, instead of using a separate input statement for each, you can specify it as @@ and provide the details.

**21: Explain the difference between FORMAT and INFORMAT.**

**Answer:**

INFORMAT is used to specify in the format in which a number should be read. It is used for input specifications. FORMAT is used to specify the printing format. It is an output specification. You can create a user-defined format using the PROC FORMAT.

**22: How is table lookup done in SAS?**

**Answer:**

SAS allows 5 types of table lookups:

a) **Direct Access** – using the SET statement, you can load one or more Data Sets directly

b) **Format Table** – the PROC Format can be used with a Data Set to load a table

c) **PROC SQL** – the PROC SQL can be used to load Data Set

d) **Arrays** – by loading the table data into an array

e) **Match Merging** – 2 lookup files and a Data Set is used up. Both lookup files are sorted by the key and the merged data goes into the Data Set.

**23: What is the function of INCLUDE command in SAS?**

**Answer:**

The INCLUDE command includes/opens a stored program in the Windows operating environment. Using include command enables us to open a stored program in the code editing window. As this is a command there is no need to add semi-colon at the end.

Suppose you want to include the program *set2.sas* which is stored in *d:\sas* you can issue the following command:

> *include 'd:\sas\set2.sas'*

## 24: What are the two categories of error commonly encountered in SAS?

**Answer:**

The two types of errors are *data errors* and *syntax errors*. Syntax errors occur when the programming statements do not comply with the rules of the language. Data errors are those errors which occur when some data values are not suitable for the SAS statements mentioned.

*Examples:*

**Syntax error** -One common example of a syntax error is missing a semi-colon at the end of a SAS statement. In the following example, semi-colon is missing in the print statement which illustrates syntax error.

*proc print data = exam.questionset2*

*run;*

**Data Error** -One common example of data error is assigning a character value to a numeric variable.

## 25: Suppose after submitting a SAS program you see the statement 'Data step running' at the top of active window. What does that indicate and how do you resolve the issue?

**Answer:**

This indicates that there is a syntax error. The error is that the data step which is submitted does not have a RUN statement. So, the data step does not execute and hence this message appears on the top of active window.

This can be resolved by submitting a RUN statement to complete the data step.

## 26: How do you specify comments in SAS?

### Answer:

There are two ways of specifying comment statements –

*\* this is a comment;*

*Or*

*/\* this is another comment\*/*


## 27: How do you invoke the debugger in SAS?

### Answer:

The debugger can be invoked by adding debug option in data statement and then executing the program.

*Example:*

*data exam.questionset2 / debug;*

   *infile exam;*

   *input one $ two $;*

*run;*

*proc print data=exam.questionset2;*

*run;*

Chapter **4**

# Reports - List and Summary

**28: What is the difference between the PRINT and REPORT commands?**

**Answer:**

PROC PRINT and PROC REPORT are both used to list the Data Set. But PROC REPORT contains a lot of options for formatting and display. PROC REPORT, by default, does not list along with the OBS number while PROC PRINT does. But you can add a computed column for printing the observation number or OBS in PROC REPORT. PROC REPORT allows you to skip/include the title, column names, resize the columns etc. While using PROC PRINT, you can sort by a particular column using the BY option. In PROC REPORT, you can sort using the ORDER option.

## 29: Explain the REPORT Procedure.

**Answer:**

The REPORT procedure is used to print or list the Data Set on screen. Using the REPORT procedure, you can specify against each column or data value whether the Data Set has to be sorted by the column, mention the variable names to be displayed against the columns, width of the column to be displayed, justify the values – left for characters and right for numeric, and the order in which the Data Set has to be displayed.

## 30: How do you select the variables and control the order in which they appear while creating a list report?

**Answer:**

This can be achieved by using VAR statement in PROC PRINT.

*Example:*

*proc print data=exam.questionset2;*

*varslno quest1 quest2 quest3;*

*run;*

## 31: How to remove the column containing observation number while creating a list report?

**Answer:**

Using NOOBS option in the PROC PRINT statement enables us to remove the column containing observation number while creating list report.

*Example:*

*proc print data=exam.questionset2 noobs;*

*var slno quest1 quest2 quest3;*

*run;*

## 32: What is the output of PROC PRINT?

**Answer:**

PROC PRINT produces a report containing a column for observation number on the left, displays all the observations and variables in the Data Set, variables in the order in which they appear in the Data Set.

## 33: How do you cancel a TITLE statement?

**Answer:**

All the previous TITLE statements can be cancelled by issuing a NULL TITLE statement or submit a TITLE1 statement with no text.

*Example:*

*title1;*

*proc print data=exam.questionset2 noobs;*

*var slno quest1 quest2 quest3;*

*run;*

The NULL TITLE1 statement causes the cancellation of all the titles which were previously defined before the execution of PROC PRINT.

## 34: Suppose you are having a Data Set *exam.questionset2*.The Data Set contains a column date. You have to assign a format (*mmddyy8.*) temporarily to the date column so that it appears in the formatted way in the output. How do you do that?

**Answer:**

This can be achieved by using the FORMAT statement. FORMAT statement is applicable only to the PROC step in which it appears.

*Example:*

*title1;*

*proc print data = exam.questionset2 noobs;*

*var slno quest1 quest2 quest3 date;*

*format date mmddyy8.;*

*run;*

## 35: How do you assign a permanent label in SAS?

**Answer:**

A permanent label can be assigned by using the LABEL statement in data step.

*Example:* The following program creates a Data Set *exam.questionset3.* Here the LABEL statement is mentioned in the data step. So, the label for the variable date is permanently assigned.

*data exam.questionset3;*

   *set exam.questionset2;*

   *label date='Finish Date';*

*run;*

*proc print data = exam.questionset3 noobs;*

*run;*

## 36: While creating a list report with PROC REPORT how do you select the variables and order them?

**Answer:**

This is achieved using COLUMN statement. COLUMN statement decides the order of variables while using PROC REPORT.

*Example:*

*proc report data = exam.questionset2 ;*

*column slno quest1 quest2 quest3 date;*

*run;*

**37: Which option is used with PROC REPORT statement to underline all column headings and space between them?**

**Answer:**

HEADLINE option can be used along with PROC REPORT for underlining all the column headings and space between them.

*Example:*

*proc report data = exam.questionset2 headline;*

*column slno quest1 quest2 quest3 date;*

*run;*

**38: What is the purpose of using ORDER option in the DEFINE statement while using PROC REPORT?**

**Answer:**

While using PROC REPORT, defining a variable as an ORDER variable produces a list report with the rows ordered according to the formatted values. PROC REPORT displays only the first occurrence of each value of an ORDER variable in a set of rows which has same value for all order variables.

The following examples produce a report from the Data Set *exam.questionset2*. DEFINE statement used below defines set as ORDER variable with label *'questionsetno'* and width of 6.So the report contains rows ordered by the variable set.

*proc report data=exam.questionset2  headline;*

*column set quest1 quest2 quest3 date;*

*define set/ order 'questionsetno' width=6;*

*run;*


## 39: Which variables are used to calculate statistics in PROC REPORT?

**Answer:**

Analysis variables are used to produce statistics in PROC REPORT. By default, all numeric variables are considered as analysis variables and used for the calculation of default statistics-sum.

# Chapter **5**

# SAS Data Sets

**40: What is the difference between DATALINES and CARDS statements?**

**Answer:**

There is no difference between DATALINES and CARDS. Earlier, when punched cards were used instead of keyboards and disks to input data, the CARDS keyword was used. Now instead, DATALINES option is used. The CARDS option is usually used with INFILE data.

**41: How do you create a permanent Data Set?**

**Answer:**

SAS allows you to create permanent and temporary Data Sets. To create a permanent Data Set, you need to first assign the library (not the WORK library) and an engine. Once the data is created, the Data Set is assigned to the library and given a name to make it permanent.

### 42: What is the function of INFILE statement?

**Answer:**

INFILE statement is used to indicate the external file in which the required data resides.

*Example:*

*infile ' D:\sas\programs\questionset1.dat' ;*

### 43: Which is the ideal situation for using COLUMN input?

**Answer:**

COLUMN input is used when data is:

a) **Standard numeric or character values:** Standard numeric data can only contain numbers, decimal points, numbers in scientific notation and plus or minus signs.

b) **In fixed columns:** For each row the values for particular field begin and end in same columns.

### 44: How do you read the data lines entered directly into the program?

**Answer:**

DATALINES statement can be used as a last statement in the data step to read the data lines directly.

*Example:*

*data exam.questionset3;*

*infile questfile;*

*input slno 1-4 author $ 5-12;*

*datalines;*

*This set contains formatted questions by famous authors*

*;*

*run;*

**45: What is the purpose of using the keyword _NULL_ in the data statement?**

**Answer:**

_NULL_ statement enables us to use the data step without creating a Data Set.

The following example uses the keyword _NULL_ to use the data step without creating a Data Set. The following example uses the keyword _NULL_ to create a raw data file by reading from the Data Set *'exam.questionset1'*.FILE statement specifies the output file location. PUT statement describes the lines to be written to the raw data file.

*data _null_;*

*set exam.questionset1;*

*file 'd:\sas\set1.dat';*

*put setno 1-4 answers5-25;*

*run;*

**46: What is the purpose of PUT statement?**

**Answer:**

The PUT statement is used to describe the data to be written to a raw data file. It is analogous to the use of input statement while reading from a raw data file.

The following example illustrates the use of PUT statement to write to a raw data file referenced by the FILEREF '*questfile*'.

*data _null_;*

   *set exam.questionset2;*

   *file questfile;*

   *put slno 1-4 author 5-12;*

*run;*

**47: Which parameters are to be mentioned in the input statement while using COLUMN input?**

**Answer:**

While using COLUMN input the input statement should contain:

   a)   SAS variable name

   b)   Type ('$' sign if it is a character column)

   c)   Starting column

   d)   Ending column if necessary

*Example:*

   *data exam.questionset3;*

      *infile questfile;*

      *input slno 1-4 author $ 5-12;*

   *run;*

**48: Usage of programming statement is one common way of creating a SAS Data Set from raw data file. What is the other way of creating SAS Data Set from a raw data file?**

**Answer:**

SAS IMPORT WIZARD is an alternate way of creating a SAS Data Set from different types of raw data files like Excel spreadsheets and text files.

**49: What is the scope of a FILENAME statement?**

**Answer:**

FILENAME statement is global. This means that the FILENAME statement remains in effect until you modify it, cancel it or end the SAS session.

**50: What is the significance of SET statement in SAS?**

**Answer:**

SET statement specifies the Data Set from which the data is to be read.

*Example:* The following program creates a Data Set *exam.questionset3* by reading the data from the Data Set *exam.questionset2*.

*data exam.questionset3;*

    *set exam.questionset2;*

    *label date='Finish Date';*

*run;*

**51: Is it possible to use date constants to assign dates in ASSIGNMENT statements?**

**Answer:**

Yes, it is possible to assign date constants.

*Example:* In the following program an ASSIGNMENT statement is used to assign a date constant to the variable *testdate*.

*data exam.questionset3;*

  *set exam.questionset2;*

  *input slno 1-3 author $ 4-12;*

  *testdate='20MAR2017'd;*

*run;*

# Chapter 6

# Data Step

**52: Explain the CONTENTS procedure.**

**Answer:**

The CONTENTS procedure lets you write the output of the SAS library or the description of one SAS Data Set. The SAS libraries contain all libraries used by SAS program including the maps, user details, work specifications etc. It contains all temporary and permanent libraries. It can be used with Data Set as a statement also. The difference is that, when used as a statement, the LIBREF is the default library whereas work is the default library for procedure.

**53: How can you optimally handle large Data Sets using SAS?**

**Answer:**

SAS can handle small as well as large Data Sets. While handling large Data Sets, SAS first requires it to be sorted by FIRSTOBS and OBS options. The COMPRESS, INDEX and BUFSIZE options help SAS to manage the large volumes of data. Compression helps to reduce the size of the observations. Index helps to locate and retrieve the observations quickly. BUFSIZE is used to mention the buffer size for storing the output.

**54: Explain the compilation phase of data step in detail.**

**Answer:**

During the compilation phase, the statements are scanned for syntax errors. If any syntax error is detected, further processing of data step is stopped. When compilation phase is complete, descriptor portion of new Data Set is created.

**55: When is an input buffer created?**

**Answer:**

Input buffer is an area of memory created to hold record from external file. Input buffer is created at the beginning of the compilation phase. It is created only when the raw data is read.

**56: Explain the automatic variable _ERROR_.**

**Answer:**

_ERROR_ is an automatic variable in program data vector. This is used to specify the error caused by data during execution. The default value is zero. This variable is not written to Data Set.

*Example:* When the following simple program is submitted, SAS processes the data step. In the compilation phase a Program Data Vector or a PDV is formed and holds observations one at a time.

This PDV contains 2- automatic variables - _ERROR _ and _N_. Also, a slot is added to the PDV for each variable in the Data Set. At the end of compilation phase, descriptor portion is created but _N_ and _ERROR_ are not written to Data Set.

*data exam.questionset3;*

    *infile exam;*

    *input slno 1-3 author $ 4-12;*

*run;*

At the beginning of execution _ERROR_ is set to zero. If there is any error during execution, like a character value being assigned to a numeric variable, the variable _ERROR_ changes to 1, indicating that an error has occurred.

**57: Explain the significance of _N_.**

**Answer:**

_N_ is an automatic variable of program data vector that tells the total number of times the data step begins to execute.

*Example:* When the following simple program is submitted, SAS processes the data step. In the compilation phase a program data vector (PDV) is created to hold observations one at a time. This PDV has 2- automatic variables - _N_ and _ERROR_. Also, a slot is added to the PDV for each variable in the Data Set. At the end of compilation phase descriptor portion is created but _N_ and _ERROR_ are not written to Data Set.

*data exam.questionset3;*

    *infile exam;*

    *input slno 1-3 author $ 4-12;*

*run;*

In the above example, SAS reads values from the file exam.
Imagine the file 'exam' contains 9 records. Data step iterates 9
times as there are 9 records in the file. During the execution all the
variables are read from file, stored in the PDV and written to the
Data Set. In this case the data step executes 9 times. While reading
first observation the value of _N_ is set to 1, for next observation
_N_ is set to 2 and so on.

**58: How do you limit the number of observations that are read
during the data step?**

**Answer:**

OBS= option can be used in the INFILE statement to limit the
number of observations that are read during the data step.

*Example:* The following program creates a new Data Set
*exam.questionset3* with all the variables but only 10 observations as
we used the option OBS=10.

*data exam.questionset3 obs=10;*

    *infile exam;*

    *input slno 1-3 author $ 4-12;*

*run;*

# Chapter **7**

# Formats

**59: What is the maximum length of label?**

**Answer:**

The label in SAS can be 256 characters long.


**60: Explain the function of the keyword FMTLIB.**

**Answer:**

FMTLIB displays the formats and values that are currently stored in the catalog.


**61: How is VALUE statement used to create formats?**

**Answer:**

VALUE statement is used to define formats for variables in the

Data Set.

*Example:* The following program creates a format -*Questfmt*. The value statement creates a format *Questfmt* to assign the descriptive labels.

*Proc format lib=library;*

    *value Questfmt*

    *1-100='initial';*

    *101-200='middle';*

    *201-300='final';*

*run;*


**62: Which keyword is used in the VALUE statement to label the missing value?**

**Answer:**

The keyword OTHER is used in the VALUE statement to label the missing values as well as unknown values.

*Example:* The following program creates a format -*Questfmt*. The VALUE statement creates a format *Questfmt* to assign the descriptive labels. The values which do not fall in the range 1-300 as well as missing/unknown values are labelled using the keyword OTHER.

*Proc format lib=library;*

    *value Questfmt*

    *1-100='initial';*

    *101-200='middle';*

    *201-300='final'*

*other='unknown';*

*run;*

Chapter **8**

# Statistics

**63: Explain Factor Analysis.**

**Answer:**

Factor Analysis comprises of the set of statements and commands used to compress the observations and summarize the Data Set. It takes into account the latent or unobserved variables that are used behind the observed variables. A minimum of 10 variables per set are required to conduct proper factor analysis. When the Priors option is set to SMC in the PROC Factor procedure, the analysis is done on a common factor model. Otherwise there are many models based on which analysis can be done.

**64: Explain PROC SUMMARY.**

**Answer:**

PROC SUMMARY can be used similar to PROC MEANS. It is used to calculate the detailed statistics on the numeric variables in a Data Set. It is also used for group calculations based on the BY clause. Even though PROC SUMMARY provides the descriptive summary of the Data Set, it does not come with a default print, so if you want the result, you have to include an explicit print statement along with PROC SUMMARY. When all variables are characters in the Data Set, the PROC SUMMARY outputs the number of observations in the output. The inclusion of VAR in PROC SUMMARY results in the same output as that of a PROC MEANS which results in N OBS, N, Mean, Standard Deviation, Minimum and Maximum.

**65: Which is the ideal procedure to use for calculating the statistics for continuous numeric variables?**

**Answer:**

PROC MEANS or PROC SUMMARY is ideal for calculating the statistics of numeric variables. Continuous numeric variables are those variables which are not discrete. Example: age of people.

The following procedure creates a report from the Data Set result with default statistics (n count, mean, standard deviation, minimum and maximum values)calculated for all numeric variables.

*proc means data = exam.result;*

*run;*

**66: What are the default statistics produced by the MEANS procedure?**

**Answer:**

MEANS procedure in its simplest form produces number of missing values, mean, standard deviation, minimum and maximum values of all numeric variables in the Data Set.

**67: Suppose you had a Data Set *exam.set1* for which you wish to calculate the median of all numeric variables. How do you use the programming statements?**

**Answer:**

This can be achieved by using MEANS procedure with the keyword MEDIAN.

*Example:*

   *proc means data= exam.set1 median;*

   *run;*

**68: Which option is used in the PROC MEANS statement to limit the number of decimal places?**

**Answer:**

MAXDEC= option is used to limit the number of decimal places in MEANS procedure.

*Example:* In the following program the option MAXDEC is set to 1. So, all the numeric variables will be having one decimal place in the report.

   *proc means data= exam.set1 maxdec=1;*

   *run;*

**69: How do you specify variables in PROC MEANS statement?**

**Answer:**

VAR statement can be used with PROC MEANS statement to

exclude certain variables and produce statistics for the desired variables.

*Example:* In the following program the VAR statement is used to include three variables - marks1, marks2, marks5. PROC MEANS produces statistics for only these variables.

> *proc means data= exam.set1 maxdec=1;*
>
> *var marks1 marks2 marks 5;*
>
> *run;*

## 70: Which statistics are generated for class variables in MEANS procedure?

**Answer:**

There are no statistics generated for class variables by PROC MEANS. The values of class variables are used for classification of data. The class variables usually contain discrete values which can be used for grouping the data.

## 71: How can you prevent the default report creation in PROC MEANS?

**Answer:**

PROC MEANS produces a report by default and this can be prevented by using the option NOPRINT.

*Example:*

> *proc means data= exam.set1 noprint;*
>
> *var markset1 markset2 markset3;*
>
> *run;*

## 72: What is the default output produced by PROC FREQ?

**Answer:**

In its simplest form PROC FREQ creates a one-way table with frequency, percent, cumulative frequency, cumulative percent of each value of all the variables in the Data Set.

## 73: How do you specify variables to be processed by PROC FREQ?

**Answer:**

TABLES statement specifies the variables to be processed by PROC FREQ.

*Example:* In the following program TABLES statement specifies the number of variables and the order in which the variables are displayed.

*proc freq data= exam.set1 ;*

*tables month setnumber;*

*run;*

## 74: Explain the significance of NOCUM option.

**Answer:**

NOCUM option is usually added to the TABLES statement to prevent the display of cumulative frequency as well as cumulative percentage in one-way frequency table.

*Example:* The addition of NOCUM option to the TABLES statement in the following program causes the frequency and percent alone to be displayed in the output.

*proc freq data= exam.set1 ;*

*tables month set / nocum;*

*run;*

### 75: What are the criteria for the data to be used for BY group processing?

**Answer:**

Data must be sorted before using BY group processing. So, it is necessary to RUN the PROC SORT before using PROC MEANS with BY statement.

### 76: What is the difference between the default output produced by PROC MEANS and PROC SUMMARY?

**Answer:**

The results which are produced by PROC MEANS and PROC SUMMARY are same. But the default output produced is different. PROC MEANS produces a report by default while PROC SUMMARY produces an output Data Set by default.

### 77: What are the default values produced when PROC FREQ is used for producing crosstabulations?

**Answer:**

The output table produced by crosstabulation has cell frequency, cell percentage of total frequency, cell percentage of row frequency and cell percentage of column frequency.

### 78: Which keyword is used with PROC MEANS to compute standard deviation?

**Answer:**

STDDEV/STD can be used with PROC MEANS to compute the

standard deviation.

*Example:*

    *proc means data= exam.set1 std;*

    *run;*


**79: How will you produce a report with PROC SUMMARY?**

**Answer:**

It is possible to produce a report along with output Data Set with PROC SUMMARY by using the option PRINT.

*Example:*

    *proc summary data= exam.set1 print;*

    *varslno set1 set2;*

    *run;*


**80: Which types of values are ideal for frequency distribution?**

**Answer:**

Categorical values/discrete values are ideal to work with frequency distribution.

*Example:* Consider the following Data Set *exam.set1*. Months are the best categorical variables as they can be used to categorize the data quickly. So, month is chosen to produce frequency tables.

*proc freq data= exam.set1 ;*

*tables month;*

*run;*

This page is intentionally left blank

# Chapter 9

# Outputs

**81: Could you list some ODS destinations which are currently supported?**

**Answer:**

HTML, LISTING, MARKUP LANGUAGES FAMILY, DOCUMENT, OUTPUT, PRINTER FAMILY and RTF are some of the ODS destinations which are currently supported by SAS.

**82: How do you use the ODS statement to open LISTING destination?**

**Answer:**

The following command can be used to open the LISTING destination.

*ods listing;*

**83: Which ODS destination is open by default?**

**Answer:**

The LISTING destination is open by default. Most destinations are closed by default and we need to open them at the beginning of the program.

**84: Which keyword is used in ODS statements to close all the open destinations at once?**

**Answer:**

_ALL_ is used in the ODS close statement to close all the open destinations at once.

*Example:* The following command will close all the open destinations at once.

  *ods _all_ close;*

**85: How does ODS handle the output?**

**Answer:**

ODS creates output objects. Output objects contain the results of steps submitted (either the data step/proc step) and information about how to display the results.

**86: How do you write the ODS statements to create a simple HTML output?**

**Answer:**

*ods html body= 'D:\ sas\examset\set1.html';*
*ods html close;*

**87: Which option is used in ODS HTML statement to specify the location of storing the output?**

**Answer:**

PATH= option can be used in ODS HTML statement to specify the location where you wish to store the HTML output.

*Example:*

*ods html path = 'C:\sas';*

  *body= 'set1.html'*

  *contents= 'set2.html'*

  *frame='set3.html';*

*proc print data= exam.questionset1;*

*run;*

*ods html close;*

This page is intentionally left blank

# Chapter **10**

# Variables

---

**88: How does the SUM statement deal with the missing values?**

**Answer:**

SUM statement is used to add the result of an expression to a variable. SUM statement ignores the missing values if an expression produces a missing value. If SUM statement encounters a missing value, then it treats the missing value as zero and continues with the calculations.

**89: How does an ASSIGNMENT statement deal with the missing values?**

**Answer:**

While using ASSIGNMENT statement, if any missing value is encountered then the ASSIGNMENT statement assigns missing value to the variable.

**90: How do you change the initial value of SUM variable?**

**Answer:**

SUM variables are initialised to zero by default. RETAIN statement can be used to change the initial value of the sum variable.

*Example:* The following program changes the initial value of the variable *setno* to 543.

*retain setno 543;*

**91: How do you consider the value of zero in SAS while using Boolean expressions?**

**Answer:**

In SAS, the value of zero and missing values are considered to be false. Any other value is true in SAS.

**92: While creating a new character variable in the ASSIGNMENT statement, how is the length of the variable determined?**

**Answer:**

While creating a new character variable in the ASSIGNMENT statement, SAS checks the first value of the variable and allocates as many bytes of storage space as required by this first value. Thus, the length of the variable will be equal to the length of first value of the variable. Remaining values of the variables are truncated or padded accordingly.

**93: Is it possible to assign length to a character variable created using ASSIGNMENT statement?**

**Answer:**

Yes, it is possible. Even though SAS allocates storage space according to the first value of the variable, it is possible to assign length using LENGTH statement.

*Example:* In the following program the variable set is assigned a length of 8 using LENGTH statement. This statement should be placed before the variable is referenced anywhere.

*length set $ 8;*

**94: What is the function of KEEP= option?**

**Answer:**

KEEP= option helps in keeping the variables required in a Data Set. Sometimes during the processing of a Data Set, it may be required to eliminate some variables and keep some. In such cases KEEP= option helps in the purpose.

**95: HOW is DROP statement used in SAS procedure?**

**Answer:**

DROP statement cannot be used with SAS procedure steps.

**96: Which form of the DO statement checks the condition before each iteration of DO loop?**

**Answer:**

In SAS, DO WHILE loop executes statements in a loop repetitively checking the condition before each iteration of the DO loop.

**97: What is the result of the following IF statement?**

if *setno*=23 or 45;

**Answer:**

The above IF statement is always true. The first condition *setno*=23 may or may not evaluate to true but 45 is always true as it is a non-missing value and not equal to zero also.

**98: Suppose you have a Data Set in which the variables are assigned with permanent labels. But, you are submitting a proc step in which you are assigning a new label to one of the variables. What will be displayed as the label for the variable- new one or the one which is permanently stored?**

**Answer:**

If we are assigning temporary labels within a proc step, they override the labels which are permanently stored in the Data Set.

# Chapter 11

# Combining Data Sets

---

**99: How do you read a Data Set *questionset1* which is stored in the library *'exam'*?**

**Answer:**

The following statement can be used to read the Data Set *questionset1* stored in the library *'exam'*:

*set exam.questionset1;*

**100: You might be aware of the DROP = option. What criteria should you use to decide whether to place the option in the SET statement or DATA statement?**

**Answer:**

DROP= option is usually used when you don't want certain variables to appear in the new Data Set. We usually specify the

DROP= option in the DATA statement if you need the variables for some processing but you don't want them to appear in the new Data Set. But if you don't require processing of certain variables and you don't want them to appear in the new Data Set also, you can use the DROP= option in the SET statement.

**101: Which variables are created automatically when you are using BY statement along with the SET statement?**

**Answer:**

Two variables are automatically created while using BY statement with SET statement, i.e.*first.variable* and *last.variable* for every variable in Data Set. These are temporary variables.

*Example:* SET statement along with BY statement. The data step creates two temporary variables:

*first.result and last.result*

*data exam.questionset1;*

*set exam.set2;*

*by result;*

*run;*

**102: How do you go straight to an observation in a Data Set without considering preceding observations?**

**Answer:**

It is possible to fetch an observation directly by using POINT= option.

Suppose you want to read 5th observation from *exam.questionset2* then we write the following:

*data exam.questionset4;*

*obs=5;*

   *set exam.questionset3 point=obs;*

*output;*

*stop;*

*run;*


## 103: What happens if we specify invalid values for POINT= variables?

**Answer:**

When SAS detects invalid values for the POINT= variable, it sets the automatic variable _ERROR_ to 1.


## 104: How do you detect an end of Data Set while reading data?

**Answer:**

To detect the end of a Data Set, a temporary numeric variable can be created with END= option in the SET statement. The variable is having a value of zero but the value changes to one when the SET statement reads the last observation from the Data Set. It is a temporary variable and is not added to the Data Set.


## 105: Which conditions have to be checked while using POINT= option?

**Answer:**

While using POINT= option, a STOP statement has to be used to prevent continuous looping. Since the observation is read directly and there is no end of the file condition reached, an output statement also needs to be used.

*Example:* Suppose you want to read 5th observation from

*exam.questionset2* then we write the following program.

*data exam.questionset4;*

*obs =5;*

*set exam.questionset3 point=obs;*

*output;*

*stop;*

*run;*

**106: While performing one-to-one reading does the resulting Data Set contain all the observations and variables from the input Data Sets?**

**Answer:**

While performing one-to-one reading, the resulting Data Set has all the variables from the input Data Sets. If the input Data Sets have variables with the same name, then the data from the Data Set which was read last overrides the data which was read earlier. The number of observations will be the same as the number of observations in the smallest Data Set.

**107: What is the maximum number of Data Sets which can be given as an input for APPEND procedure?**

**Answer:**

While using APPEND procedure, only two Data Sets can be combined at a time.

**108: How does concatenating combine the input Data Sets?**

**Answer:**

When a program is submitted to concatenate two or more data

sets, SAS first reads all the observations from the first Data Set. Then it proceeds to next Data Set, reads all the observations and variables and so on. Thus, the new Data Set which is produced after concatenation will have all the observations and variables from the combining Data Sets.

*Example:* The following Data Set *exam.questionset4* contains all the observations and variables from both set2 and set3.

*data exam.questionset4;*

*set exam.set2 exam.set3;*

*run;*

**109: What is the prerequisite for two Data Sets to be merged by MERGE statement?**

**Answer:**

The two Data Sets must be either indexed or sorted according to the variables mentioned as BY variables. Also, each BY variable must be having the same data type in all the input Data Sets.

**110: How do you use the RENAME Data Set option?**

**Answer:**

RENAME= data option is used with SET or MERGE statement. It can also be used in the data statement.

The syntax is as follows:

(RENAME = (current variable name= new variable name))

**111: How many variables can be renamed at one time using RENAME= option?**

**Answer:**

Any number of variables can be renamed at one stretch using RENAME= option.

### 112: How does one-to-one merging produce output?

**Answer:**

As the name implies one-to-one merging is identical to one-to one reading but there are some differences. The output Data Set produced by one-to-one merging contains all the observations and variables from the input Data Sets. Also, one-to-one merging uses MERGE statement rather than multiple SET statements.

### 113: What is the functionality of IN= Data Set option?

**Answer:**

IN= Data Set option is used in match-merging process to avoid those observations which do not match. This creates a temporary variable and based on the value of the variable, those observations which do not match in the two Data Sets (un-matching observations) are excluded.

### 114: What is the difference between PROC APPEND and CONCATENATE?

**Answer:**

The results produced by both PROC APPEND and CONCATENATE look identical. But CONCATENATE produces a new Data Set with all the observations and variables from the input Data Sets. PROC APPEND simply adds the observations and variables from one Data Set to the base Data Set. PROC APPEND does not read the base Data Set and it does not produce a new Data Set as well.

*Example:* The following program concatenates two Data Sets and produces a new Data Set *exam.questionset4* which contains all the observations and variables from the input Data Sets.

   *data exam.questionset4;*

      *set exam.set2 exam.set3;*

   *run;*

The following program appends the observations in set3 to the end of observations in set2. No new Data Set is produced.

   *proc append base=exam.set2;*

      *data= exam.set3;*

   *run;*

**115: In which scenarios do you prefer to use the Data Set option KEEP = rather than using the Data Set option DROP=?**

**Answer:**

The Data Set options KEEP = and DROP = are used for specifying the variable to be included or dropped. KEEP = option is generally used when more number of variables are to be dropped. In such cases, the number of variables to be maintained will be less; so it will be easy to list those variables with KEEP= option.

This page is intentionally left blank

# Chapter **12**

# SAS Functions

---

**116: Which function is used to convert character data values to numeric data values?**

**Answer:**

INPUT function converts character data values to numeric data values. Syntax of the function is *input(source, INFORMAT)*. *source* is the character variable or constant which needs to be converted to numeric data values. INFORMAT should be numeric to read the form of the values.

*Example:* The following program converts the character variable 'set' to numeric values. set is the source and it has a length of 3. So, a numeric INFORMAT of 3. is used to read the values of the variable 'set'. When the data step is executed, a new numeric variable type is created.

*data exam.questionset4;*

```
set exam.set3;

type= input(set, 3.);

run;
```

## 117: How does SAS store a date value?

**Answer:**

SAS stores date value as number of days from January 1, 1960 to the given date.

*Example:* Jan 1, 1961 is counted as 366 days by SAS.

## 118: Explain the significance of the function MDY.

**Answer:**

MDY is a function which is used to create a date. It takes month, day and year as input and returns a date value.

*Example:* The following program uses MDY function to create a date from the input values. The function calculates the date value, March 27, 2012 and assigns it to date variable.

```
data exam.questionset4;

    set exam.set3;

date= mdy(3, 27, 2012);

run;
```

## 119: What is the significance of DATE function?

**Answer:**

DATE function returns the current date as a SAS date value. The DATE function requires no arguments.

*Example:* When the following data step is submitted, a new

variable *'mydate'* is created. *'mydate'* contains the value of current date.

> *data exam.questionset4;*
>
>> *setexam.set3;*
>
> *mydate= date();*
>
> *run;*

**120: Which function can be used interchangeably with DATE function?**

**Answer:**

TODAY function can be used interchangeably with DATE function. TODAY also returns the current date as a SAS date value. TODAY function requires no arguments.

*Example:* When the following data step is submitted, a new variable *'mydate'* is created. *'mydate'* contains the value of current date.

> *data exam.questionset4;*
>
>> *set exam.set3;*
>
> *mydate= today();*
>
> *run;*

**121: Name some functions which provide results which are analogous to the results produced by any SAS procedure like PROC MEANS.**

**Answer:**

SUM, MEAN, MIN, MAX, VAR are some of the functions which produce the same result which is produced by PROC MEANS.

The following example illustrates the use of one of the above function - SUM. When the following data step is submitted, a new variable *'value'* is created. *'value'* contains the sum of three variables.

```
data exam.questionset4;
   set exam.set3;
value= sum(x1, x2,x3);
run;
```

### 122: What is a target variable?

**Answer:**

Target variable is a variable to which the result of the function is assigned.

*Example:* In the following program the result of the DATE function is assigned to a variable *'mydate'*. Hence *'mydate'* is the target variable.

```
data exam.questionset4;
   set exam.set3;
mydate= date();
run;
```

### 123: What happens when a character value is used in arithmetic operations?

**Answer:**

When a character value is used in arithmetic operations, SAS does an automatic conversion of the character value to numeric value. After the completion of automatic conversion, a message is written to the log indicating that automatic conversion has occurred.

*Example:* In the following program, 'set' is a character variable. But when it is used in arithmetic operation (multiplication), SAS does an automatic conversion of character values into numeric values.

    *data exam.questionset4;*

      *set exam.set3;*

    *type= set\*3;*

    *run;*

**124: Is the automatic conversion of character value to numeric and vice versa permissible in WHERE statements?**

**Answer:**

WHERE statement does not support automatic conversion. Whenever there occurs a mismatch in the WHERE comparisons, automatic conversion is not performed. SAS stops the processing and error statements are written to SAS log.

Here in the below example a character value of '453' is assigned to the variable '*type*'. But in the WHERE statement a numeric value is compared which is a wrong data type. Here an automatic conversion does not occur; instead SAS stops processing the program and error message is written to the log.

    *data exam.questionset4;*

      *set exam.set3;*

    *type= '453';*

    *run;*

    *proc print data=exam.questionset4;*

    *where type=453;*

    *run;*

**125: Which function is used to extract the quarter of the year in which a given date is falling?**

**Answer:**

The function QTR is used to extract the quarter of the year from a given date.

*Example:* In the following program QTR function is used to extract the quarter values from the variable *'start date'* which holds the date values.

```
data exam.questionset4;
  set exam.set3;
set= qtr(startdate);
run;
```

**126: Explain the significance of the function WEEKDAY.**

**Answer:**

The function WEEKDAY is used to extract day of week from a given date. WEEKDAY function returns a number from 1 to 7 where, 1 corresponds to Sunday, 2 corresponds to Monday and so on.

*Example:* In the following program WEEKDAY function is used to extract the day of week from the variable, start date, which holds the date values.

```
data exam.questionset4;
  set exam.set3;
set= weekday(startdate);
run;
```

## 127: Explain INTCK function in detail.

**Answer:**

The function INTCK is used to count the number of time intervals within a specified period. The interval is specified by a character variable and it can be day, weekday, month, quarter, year etc.

*Example:* In the following program INTCK function creates a new variable, year, and assigns a value of 2 as 2 years have been elapsed between 27 mar 2012 and 27 mar 2014.

*data exam.questionset4;*

*set exam.set3;*

*years=intck('year','27mar2012'd, '27mar2014'd, );*

*run;*

## 128: Which function is used to extract an integer value from a given numeric value?

**Answer:**

INT function can be used to extract the integer portion of a numeric value. The argument of an integer function can be numeric variable, constant or expression.

*Example:* The following program creates a variable *result1*. The INT function extracts the integer portion of numeric variable result and assigns it to *result1*.

*data exam.questionset4;*

*set exam.set3;*

*result1= int(result)*

*run;*

## 129: What happens when you specify an invalid date as an argument in MDY function?

**Answer:**

If the argument in MDY function is specified as invalid, then MDY function assigns missing value to the target variable.

*Example:* The following program uses MDY function to create a date from the input values. Here the date specified is invalid as the month is shown to be 36 so a missing value will be assigned to the *date* variable.

*data exam.questionset4;*

  *setexam.set3;*

*date= mdy(36, 27, 2012);*

*run;*

## 130: Explain INTNX function in detail.

**Answer:**

The INTNX function performs calculations with date values, time values and datetime values. INTNX function increments date, time or datetime values by intervals and returns the result. Intervals can be day, weekday, month, quarter, semi year and year.

*Example:* In the following program INTNX function creates a new variable year and assigns a value corresponding to January 1, 2015.

*data exam.questionset4;*

  *setexam.set3;*

*year=intnx('year','03mar2012'd,3);*

*run;*

## 131: What is the functionality of TRIM function?

**Answer:**

The TRIM function helps in removing the trailing blanks from character values. It generally takes character variables as input argument. It is also possible to nest other functions within TRIM function. The following program illustrates the use of TRIM function. TRIM function removes the trailing blanks from the values of the variable *'quest'* and assigns it to the new variable *'newquest'*.

*data exam.questionset4;*

*set exam.set3;*

*newquest=trim(quest);*

*run;*

## 132: Which function converts all the letters of a character expression to uppercase?

**Answer:**

UPCASE function is used for converting all the letters of character to uppercase. The following program illustrates the use of UPCASE function. UPCASE function converts all the characters in the variable *'question'* to uppercase and assigns it to *'newquestion'*.

*data exam.questionset4;*

*set exam.set3;*

*newquestion=upcase(question);*

*run;*

### 133: Is TRANWRD a character function? Explain the functionality.

**Answer:**

TRANWRD function is a character function. It enables us to replace a pattern of characters within a string with any desired pattern of characters. In the following example, TRANWRD function is used to update the variable name. It has three arguments- *'name'*, the source in which function needs to operate, *'cat'*, the target which needs to be searched in source and *'pet'*, the pattern which needs to replace cat. When the below data step is submitted all the occurrences of *'cat'* gets replaced by *'pet'* in the variable *'name'*.

*data exam.questionset4;*

*set exam.set3;*

*name= tranwrd(name, 'cat','pet');*

*run;*

### 134: Which function enables you to search any string within a character variable?

**Answer:**

INDEX function enables to search any string within a character variable. If the string is found, then it returns the position of first character of the string. If it is not found, it returns zero. The following example illustrates the use of INDEX function. *'name'* is the variable in which the INDEX function looks for the occurrence of the string *'cat'*. If it finds the string *'cat'* then it returns the position of first character of *'cat'*. If no match is found, it returns zero. Consider a situation where in one of the values of the variable name is *concat*. In such scenario the INDEX function returns the letter 4 as it is the starting position of first character of 'cat'.

```
data exam.questionset4;
   setexam.set3;
  name1= index (name, 'cat',);
  run;
```

## 135: Name one function which is used to concatenate the strings in SAS.

**Answer:**

CATX function enables us to concatenate the strings in SAS. CATX function also removes the leading or trailing blanks and inserts separators in the new value. The input parameters specified in CATX function are the strings and separator which we wish to put in the new value.

The following example illustrates the use of CATX function. CATX function concatenates two strings *'lastname'* and *'firstname'* and assigns it to the variable *'newname'*. The separator used is *','* which indicates that in the new variable *'newname'*, the values of *'lastname'* and *'firstname'* are separated by comma.

```
data exam.questionset4;
   set exam.set3;
  newname= catx(',',lastname, firstname,);
  run;
```

## 136: What is the functionality of SCAN function?

**Answer:**

Suppose you have a character value, marked by delimiters and you wish to split the value into separate words. SCAN function is used primarily to achieve this and return a specified word.

The following example illustrates the use of SCAN function.

SCAN function is used to extract the value of last name from the variable '*name*'. The values in the variable name are comma separated. So, comma is specified as an input argument in the SCAN function. 1 is specified to indicate that the first word of the variable *name* should be extracted.

> *data exam.questionset4;*
>
> > *setexam.set3;*
>
> *lastname= scan(name, 1,',');*
>
> *run;*

### 137: Explain the significance of PROPCASE function.

**Answer:**

PROPCASE function is used to convert all the words in the argument to proper case. Proper case means that first letter of each word is capitalized.

The following example illustrates the use of PROPCASE function. PROPCASE function takes the variable 'result' as input argument and converts it to proper case and assigns it to the variable '*newresult*'. The first letter of each word in the values of '*newresult*' is capitalized.

> *data exam.questionset4;*
>
> > *set exam.set3;*
>
> *newresult= propcase(result);*
>
> *run;*

**138: What is the output of DAY function in SAS?**

**Answer:**

DAY function returns the day of the month (1-31) for a given date i.e. when a date value is given as an argument to the DAY function, it checks the corresponding day. If the date is 4th April 2012, it returns the value 4.

*Example:* In the following program DAY function is used to extract the day values from the variable *'startdate'* which holds the date values.

*data exam.questionset4;*

*setexam.set3;*

*set= day(startdate);*

*run;*

**139: What is the default length which SCAN function assigns to the target variable?**

**Answer:**

SCAN function assigns a length of 200 to each target variable.

**140: Explain functionality of SUBSTR function.**

**Answer:**

SUBSTR function is used to extract any number of characters from a string, starting from a specified position in the string.

The following example illustrates the use of SUBSTR function. SUBSTR function is used to extract the value of a character string. As the position (second argument) is 1, the extraction starts from the first position. The third argument, number of characters to be extracted is defined as 3 which indicates that 3 letter word is to be extracted. So here SUBSTR function extracts first 3 letters from the variable month and assigns it to the variable *'newmonth'*.

```
data exam.questionset4;

  set exam.set3;

newmonth= substr(month,1,3);

run;
```

Chapter **13**

# DO Loops

**141: How do you construct a basic DO loop in SAS or explain the syntax of DO loop.**

**Answer:**

DO loop helps in reducing the number of statements while performing repeated calculations. The syntax of DO loop is as follows:

*DO <index variable>=<start>TO <stop>BY <increment>;*

*SAS statements;*

*END;*

Here, the *increment, start* and *stop* can be numerals, variables or expressions in SAS.

The following example shows the calculation of *'sum'* variable using DO loop. *'count'* is index variable which gets incremented from 1 to 12. *'sum'* statement executes 12 times within the DO loop for every iteration of the data step.

```
data exam.questionset4;
  sum=0;
do count=1 to 12 by 1;
sum+1;
end;
run;
```

## 142: What is the default increment value in DO loop?

**Answer:**

If we do not state a BY condition in DO loop, default increment value is 1.

The following example shows the calculation of sum variable using DO loop. *'count'* is index variable which gets incremented from 1 to 12 .*'sum'* statement executes 12 times within the DO loop for every iteration of data step. There is no BY clause specified but the count variable gets incremented by 1.

```
data exam.questionset4;
  sum=0;
do count=1 to 12 ;
sum+1;
end;
run;
```

## 143: Can DO loops be used to combine DATA and PROC steps?
**Answer:**

DO loops are data step statements and cannot be used along with PROC steps.

**144: In SAS is it allowed to decrement DO loop?**

**Answer:**

It is possible to decrement a DO loop, by selecting a negative number for BY clause.

The following example shows the use of negative BY clause. Index variable gets decremented from 10 to 1. *'sum'* statement gets executed 10 times within DO loop for every iteration of data step.

*data exam.questionset4;*

*sum=0;*

*do count=10 to 1 by -1 ;*

*sum+1;*

*end;*

*run;*

**145: While specifying the number of iterations in DO loop in SAS, is it possible to list the items in series?**

**Answer:**

It is possible to list the items in series to specify the number of iterations of DO loop. Commas can be used to separate the items in series. When DO loop is executing, it executes for every item in its series. The items should be all character or all numeric or all variable names.

In the following example, items are listed in a series. When DO loop executes, it executes for every item in its series. Here all the items are numeric, and the below loop executes for 5 times.

```
data exam.questionset4;
  sum=0;
do count=3, 7, 9, 13, 20;
sum+1;
end;
run;
```

**146: Which condition has to be taken care of while specifying variable names to specify the number of iterations in DO loop?**

**Answer:**

While specifying variable names to specify the number of iterations in DO loop, it should be noted that the names of variables should be either all character or all numeric. SAS allows only one type of variable names in a single loop. Also, variable names should not be in quotation marks.

In the following example, items are listed in a series. When DO loop executes, it executes for every item in its series. Here all the items (*set1*, *set2*, *set3*) are numeric and the below loop executes for 3 times.

```
data exam.questionset4;
  sum=0;
do count=set1, set2, set3;
sum+1;
end;
run;
```

## 147: How does a DO UNTIL loop execute in SAS?

**Answer:**

DO UNTIL loop executes a DO loop until an expression is found to be true. The expression is evaluated at the end of the loop. So, DO UNTIL loop is executed at least once. It executes until the expression is true.

The following example illustrates the usage of DO UNTIL loop. The following loop executes 11 times until the value of sum becomes 11, after which it stops.

*data exam.questionset4;*

  *sum=0;*

*do until (sum>10);*

*sum+1;*

*end;*

*run;*

## 148: Explain the DO WHILE loop.

**Answer:**

DO WHILE loop statement also executes DO loop based on a condition. Here the condition is checked at the beginning of the loop. So, the loop executes only if the state is true. If the output in the DO WHILE loop is found to be false, this loop will not execute.

The following example illustrates the usage of DO WHILE loop. Since this is a DO WHILE loop, condition is checked at the beginning of the loop. The condition is false, since the value of sum is 0. So, the below loop will not execute.

*data exam.questionset4;*

```
sum=0;
do while (sum>10);
sum+1;
end;
run;
```

## 149: How do you create observation for every iteration of a DO loop?

**Answer:**

It is possible to create observation for every iteration of a DO loop by placing output statements inside the DO loop.

In the following example, placing an explicit output statement causes observation for every iteration of DO loop to be written to the Data Set. In the absence of this output statement, only the final observation would be written to the Data Set.

```
data exam.questionset4;
sum=0;
do until (sum>10);
sum+1;
output;
end;
run;
```

## 150: Is it possible to nest DO loops in SAS?

**Answer:**

It is possible to nest the DO loops in SAS. Putting one DO loop inside other loop is called nesting of DO loops. It should be taken care that index variable should be different in each DO loop and each DO loop should be ended properly with an end statement.

In the following example, the variables sum, and result are initialized to zero. The first loop executes five times incrementing the value of sum. For every iteration of the outer loop, the inner DO loop executes 10 times.

```
data exam.questionset4;
    sum=0;
    result=0;
    do count=1 to 5 ;
        sum+1;
            do index=1 to 10;
                result+1;
            end;
        end;
run;
```

This page is intentionally left blank

# Chapter **14**

# Arrays

---

**151: What is the scope of an array in SAS?**

**Answer:**

An Array stores multiple values under the same name. It is otherwise known as a collection of values identified by the same name. An array will exist only while the data step is in use. The scope of the array is the same as that of data step associated with it.

**152: What will happen if you name an array with a function name?**

**Answer:**

If an array is given the same name as a function name, the array will function correctly, but it won't be possible to use the function in the same data step in which array is defined. A warning message will appear in the log.

### 153: In SAS, is it possible to use array names in DROP, KEEP, LENGTH and FORMAT statements?

**Answer:**

No, SAS does not allow you to specify array names in DROP, KEEP, LENGTH and FORMAT statements.

### 154: How do you define a one-dimensional array?

**Answer:**

An array can be defined by using an ARRAY statement. An ARRAY statement contains the name of the array, dimension of the array and the elements to be included in the array. The dimension indicates the number of elements in the array and their arrangements.

In the following example, an array result is created which has a dimension of 5. It has five numeric elements *set1*, *set2*, *set3*, *set4* and *set5*.

  *data exam.questionset4;*

   *set exam.questionset3;*

     *array result {5} set1 set2 set3 set4 set5;*

  *run;*

### 155: How do you indicate the dimension of a one-dimensional array?

**Answer:**

The dimension of a one-dimensional array can be specified as a number in the ARRAY statement. It is also possible to specify the dimension by including an asterisk{*} in the ARRAY statement. While using asterisk you need to specify the elements to be included so that SAS determines the number of elements by counting them.

In the following example, an array result is created which has a dimension of 5. It has five numeric elements *set1, set2, set3, set4* and *set5*.

> *data exam.questionset4;*
>
>> *set exam.questionset3;*
>>
>>> *array result {5} set1 set2 set3 set4 set5;*
>>>
>>> */\* array result {\*} set1 set2 set3 set4 set5;\*/*
>
> *run;*

**156: Which term do you use to specify that the array includes all the numeric variables which are defined in the current data step?**

**Answer:**

_NUMERIC_ should be used in the ARRAY statement to specify that all the numeric variables are to be included in the array.

In the following example, an array result is created with all numeric variables used in the data step.

> *data exam.questionset4;*
>
>> *set exam.questionset3;*
>>
>>> *array result {\*} _numeric_;*
>
> *run;*

**157: Which function is used to determine number of elements in an array?**

**Answer:**

DIM function returns the number of elements in an array. It takes input parameter as an array name. It can be used as a counter in the DO loop as well.

In the following example, an array result is created with an ARRAY statement. DIM function is used to determine the stop value in the DO loop. The DIM function returns a value of 5 as there are five elements in the array result.

```
data exam.questionset4;

  set exam.questionset3;

    array result {*}  set1 set2 set3 set4 set5;

    do count=1 to dim(result);

      result{i}= result{i}*2;

    end;

run;
```

**158: How do you define an array of character variables in SAS?**

**Answer:**

An array of character variables can be defined by adding a $ sign in the array statement.

In the following example, a character array result is created with an ARRAY statement. The array has five elements.

```
data exam.questionset4;

  set exam.questionset3;

    array result {5} $   set1 set2 set3 set4 set5;
```

```
    do count=1 to dim(result);
        result{i}= result{i}*2;
    end;
run;
```

**159: How do you assign initial values to the array element?**

**Answer:**

It is possible to assign initial values to the array elements using the ARRAY statement.

In the following example, an array result is created with an ARRAY statement. The array has five elements. The initial values of each of the five elements are set to 100, 200, 300, 400 and 500.

```
data exam.questionset4;
    set exam.questionset3;
        array result {5} set1 set2 set3 set4 set5 (100 200 300 400 500);
        do count=1 to dim(result);
            result{i}= result{i}*2;
        end;
run;
```

**160: How do you define a two-dimensional array?**

**Answer:**

It is possible to define a two-dimensional array by specifying the number of elements in both the dimension in the ARRAY statement. The first dimension specifies the number of rows and second dimension specifies the number of columns.

In the following example, a two-dimensional array result is

created with an ARRAY statement. The array has six elements.

The array elements are grouped into 2 rows and 3 columns. They are grouped according to the order in which they are listed. *set1, set2, set3* form the first row and remaining i.e. *set4, set5* and *set6* form the second row.

> *data exam.questionset4;*
>
> > *set exam.questionset3;*
> >
> > > *array result {2,3}   set1 set2 set3 set4 set5 set6;*
> >
> > *run;*

# Chapter **15**

# Raw Data

---

**161: Define nonstandard numeric data.**

**Answer:**

Nonstandard numeric data can be defined as the data which contains:

a) special characters such as percentage signs, dollar signs and commas

b) date value or time value

c) data in fraction, binary and hexadecimal form

**162: What is free format data?**

**Answer:**

Free format data is unorganized data or data that is not stored in columns of specific length and type. Its values never start and end in the same column.

The following shows an example of a part of free format data. Note that the values of the fields do not end and begin in the same column.

| author1 | author2 | value |
|---------|---------|--------|
| Charles | James | 255000 |
| Dickenson | Thomas | 55555 |
| Cameroon | Bill | 5000 |

**163: Which features of COLUMN input allow it to be used for reading raw data?**

**Answer:**

COLUMN input has several features which enables it to be used for reading raw data. They are as follows:

a) It can be used to read the character values which contain embedded blanks.

b) A blank field is considered as a missing value. It does not cause other fields to be read incorrectly.

c) Fields need not be always separated by blanks or other delimiters.

d) Fields can be re-read. Also, parts of fields can be re-read.

**164: Which are the two input styles which SAS uses for reading data in fixed fields?**

**Answer:**

SAS uses two input styles - COLUMN input and formatted input for reading data in fixed fields. COLUMN input is used to read standard data in fixed fields while formatted input can be used to read both standard and non-standard data.

The following example illustrates the use of COLUMN input. The input statement reads the value of the variable *'slno'* which is spread from column 1 to column 4. Next it moves the pointer to column 5 and the values of the column author is read which in turn occupies column 5 to column 12.

**COLUMN input**

*data exam.questionset3;*

   *infile questfile;*

*input slno 1-4 author $ 5-12;*

*run;*

The following example illustrates the use of formatted input while reading the raw data with @ pointer control. The input statement reads the value of the variable *'slno'* at column 1. Next @ pointer control moves the pointer to column 5 and the values of the column *author* is read.

**Formatted input**

*data exam.questionset3;*

   *infile questfile;*

*input  @1 slno 4. @5 author $ 7.;*

*run;*

**165: Which parameters are to be mentioned in the input statement while using formatted input?**

**Answer:**

Formatted input enables us to read both standard and nonstandard data in fixed fields. The following parameters are to be included while using formatted input:

a) **Column pointer control:** They are of two types- @n which moves the pointer to a specific column number indicated by the value of n and +n which moves the input pointer relative to the current column.

b) **Variable name:** Variable name which is to be created in the Data Set after reading the raw file.

c) **INFORMAT:** This specifies how the data is read.

The following example illustrates the use of formatted input while reading the raw data with two pointer controls. The first program uses @ pointer control while second program uses + pointer control. The input statement reads the value of the variable *'slno'* at column 1. Next @ pointer control moves the pointer to column 5 and the values of the column *author* is read.

**Formatted input using @ pointer control**

*data exam.questionset3;*

   *infile questfile;*

*input @1 slno 4. @5 author $ 7.;*

*run;*

The following example illustrates the use of formatted input while reading the raw data using + pointer control. The input statement reads the value of the variable *'slno'* at column 1. After the values of *'slno'* are read the column pointer is moved 1 column ahead (+1) to read the values of *author*.

**Formatted input using + pointer control**

*data exam.questionset3;*

*infile questfile;*

   *input @1 slno 4. +1 author $ 7.;*

*run;*

**166: Which numeric INFORMAT can be used if the data contains commas, percentage signs, dashes and dollars?**

**Answer:**

*COMMAw.d Informat* can be used to read the numeric values and it also removes embedded blanks, commas, dashes and dollar sign. The *COMMAw.d Informat* has 3 parts:

a) Name of the INFORMAT which is comma
b) Value which is used to specify the width of the field followed by the period
c) Value which is used to indicate the number of decimal places

*Example: COMMA9.2 Informat* can be used to read the nonstandard numeric data with width of 9 and containing 2 decimal places.

**167: What is fixed length record format?**

**Answer:**

An external file can have different types of record format. Record format specifies how records are arranged in an external file. Fixed length records are one type of record format. External files with fixed length record format have an end of record marker after certain fixed number of columns. Normal record length in external files is usually 80 columns.

**168: Describe the significance of PAD option.**

**Answer:**

PAD option is usually used to avoid the problems while reading variable length records using column/formatted input. The PAD option can be specified in the INFILE statement and it pads each of the records with blanks so that all the records in the external file have same length.

The following example illustrates the use of formatted input reading an external file specified by the FILEREF *'questfile'* with PAD option. Since the file has variable record length, PAD option pads each of the records with blanks so that all are of same length. This is particularly useful when there are missing values at the end of each record.

**Formatted input using @ pointer control**

*data exam.questionset3;*

*    infile questfile;*

*input @1 slno 4. @5 author $ 7.;*

*run;*

**169: Which parameters are to be mentioned in the input statement while using LIST input?**

**Answer:**

LIST input is used for reading standard as well as nonstandard free format data. The following parameters are to be used in the input statement while reading the data with LIST input:

a) **Variable name:** specifies the variable name whose value is to be read

b) **$:** This specifies that the variable is character. This is used only while reading character variables.

The following example illustrates the use of LIST input while reading raw data.

**LIST input**

*data exam.questionset3;*

*infile questfile;*

*input slno author$ ;*

*run;*

**170: Explain the significance of DLM= option.**

**Answer:**

DLM= option is used in the INFILE statement to specify any other delimiter other than blank. Blank is the default delimiter. So, it is always advisable to specify the usage of any other delimiter.

The following example illustrates the use of DLM= option. Comma is specified as a delimiter. Any number of characters up to 200 can be used to specify delimiters.

*data exam.questionset3;*

*infile questfile dlm=',';*

*input slno author$ ;*

*run;*

**171: Is it possible to specify a range of character variables in the input statement, if the values are sequential?**

**Answer:**

Yes, it is possible to specify a range of character variables in the input statement if the values of the variables are sequential. While using LIST input to read these values, both the range of character variables and dollar sign must be enclosed in parenthesis.

In the following example, the input statement creates 5-character variables- *author1, author2, author3, author4* and *author5.*

*data exam.questionset3;*

*infile quest file dlm=',';*

*input (author1-author5) ($) ;*

*run;*


## 172: What are the main limitations of LIST input?

**Answer:**

LIST input when used in default form has many limitations:

a)  Data should be standard numeric/character.

b)  Character values must not contain embedded delimiters.

c)  Character values which are longer than 8 characters will get truncated.

d)  Missing values must be represented by some character like period.


## 173: Which option enables you to read the missing values at the end of the record?

**Answer:**

MISSOVER option can be used in the INFILE statement to read the missing values at the end of the record. Without MISSOVER option in the INFILE statement, the LIST input goes to next record if it does not find values for all the variables in the current line. MISSOVER option prevents SAS from going to next record in such cases and values which are not found are set to missing.

The following example illustrates the use of MISSOVER option. MISSOVER option prevents SAS from going to next record if it does not find values for all the variables in the current record. Values which are not found are set to missing. Thus, MISSOVER option enables to read the missing values at the end of the record.

*data exam.questionset3;*

*infile questfile missover;*

*input slno author$ ;*

*run;*

**174: Which option is specified to read the missing values at the beginning or middle of the record?**

**Answer:**

DSD option can be used in the INFILE statement to read the missing values at the middle of the record. DSD option also enables you to read the missing values at the beginning of the record provided a delimiter precedes a first value in the record.

The following example illustrates the use of DSD option. DSD enables to read the missing values at the beginning or the middle of the record.

*data exam.questionset3;*

*infile questfile dsd;*

*input slno author$ ;*

*run;*

**175: How does the DSD option affect the way SAS treats delimiters when used with LIST input?**

**Answer:**

DSD option affects the way SAS treats delimiters when used with LIST input in the following ways:

a) DSD option sets the default delimiter to comma.

b) It treats two consecutive delimiters as a missing value and thus, helps in identifying the missing values in between the record.

c) It helps in removing the quotation marks from the values.

**176: What happens when LIST input is used to read character variables whose value has length more than 8?**

**Answer:**

When LIST input is used to read the values of character variables whose value has length more than 8, the values of the variables get truncated to 8 when they are written to program data vector and after that to Data Set.

The above limitation can be overcome by writing a "LENGTH statement" preceding the input statement.

*Example:* In the following program the LENGTH statement which precedes the input statement defines the length and type for the character variable- *author*. A length of 20 has been assigned to the variable *'author'*. Since LENGTH statement has been added in the following program, even those values of the *'author'* which are longer than 8 characters are correctly read into the Data Set. In the absence of LENGTH statement those values of *'author'* which are greater than 8 characters will get truncated to 8.

*data exam.questionset3;*

   *infile questfile dsd;*

*length author $ 20;*

*input slno author$ ;*

*run;*

**177: Which modifier is used with LIST input to read the character values having embedded blanks?**

**Answer:**

LIST input can be made more versatile by modifying it. An ampersand (&) modifier can be used with LIST input to read the values of character variables with embedded blanks.

*Example:* In the following program the LENGTH statement which precedes the input statement defines the length and type for the character variable- *author*. The variable *'author'* may contain values with embedded blanks like Charles Dickens. Use of '&' modifier enables us to read the value of *'author'* which contains embedded blanks.

*data exam.questionset3;*

*  infile questfile dsd;*

*length author $ 20;*

*input slno author& ;*

*run;*

### 178: Which modifier is used along with LIST input to read the nonstandard data values?

**Answer:**

LIST input can be made more versatile by modifying it. A colon (:) modifier can be used with LIST input to read the non-standard data values which are not having embedded blanks.

*Example:* In the following program *'value'* is a field which contains non-standard numeric values like comma and does not contain embedded blanks. So, the colon (:) modifier when used in the input statement enables us to read the values of the variable *'value'* properly using an INFORMAT comma.

*data exam.questionset3;*

*  infile questfile dsd;*

*length author $ 20;*

*input slno author & value : comma. ;*

*run;*

## 179: How does an INFORMAT function when used with formatted input?

**Answer:**

INFORMAT works in a different way when used with modified LIST input compared to when used with formatted input. When used as formatted input, INFORMAT determines the length of a variable as well as the number of columns which are being read.

*Example:* The following example illustrates the use of formatted input while reading raw data with @ pointer control. The input statement reads the value of the variable *'author'*. Here an INFORMAT 7. is used to read the values of the variable *'author'*. Input statement reads 7 columns from each record.

**Formatted input**

*data exam.questionset3;*

  *infile questfile;*

*input  @1 slno 4. @5 author $ 7.;*

*run;*

## 180: How does an INFORMAT function work when used with modified LIST input?

**Answer:**

INFORMAT works in a different way when used with modified LIST input compared to when used with formatted input. The INFORMAT in modified LIST input checks only the length of the variable and does not check the number of columns which are being read.

*Example:* In the following program the INFORMAT used ($12.) checks only the length of the variable *'author'*. Here the raw data values are read till 2-successive blanks are found.

*data exam.questionset3;*

  *infile questfile dsd;*

*length author $ 20;*

*input slno author & $12. ;*

*run;*

**181: What all parameters must be mentioned while using PUT statement with LIST output?**

**Answer:**

The PUT statement can be used along with LIST output to create free format raw data files. The following parameters are to be included:

a) **Variable name:** Variable specifies which variable you need to write to raw data file

b) **: (colon):** colon is specified before a format (it is optional and used only when format is specified)

c) **format:** This specifies which format to use for writing the values to the raw data file

*Example:* In the following program a raw data file *'questfile'* is created using the Data Set *exam.questionset3*. The program illustrates the use of PUT statement. date9. format is used for writing the variable *'startdate'*.

*data _null_ ;*

*set exam.questionset3;*

*file 'c:\sas\questfile';*

*put slno  author  startdate : date9.;*

*run;*


**182: Is it allowed to mix three types of input styles to read the raw data?**

**Answer:**

Yes, it is allowed to mix three types of input styles - COLUMN input, formatted input and LIST input in order to read the raw data. Infact, to read some types of raw data files, it is required to mix three types of input styles.

*Example:* In the following program three types of input styles are mixed to read from a raw data file. In the raw data file, the values of *'slno'* are standard and data are located in fixed columns. So, COLUMN input is used to read the values of the variable *'slno'*. The field *'author'* is also standard but this requires an INFORMAT. So, formatted input is used to read the values of the variable *'author'*. The third field *'startdate'* does not begin or end in the same column. So, LIST input is used to read the values of *'startdate'*.

*data exam.questionset3;*

*    infile questfile dsd;*

*length author $ 20;*

*input  slno 1-3 @5 author  $12. startdate : date9. ;*

*run;*

**183: How do you use a PUT statement to write a character string to a raw data file?**

**Answer:**

It is possible to write a character string to a raw data file using PUT statement by adding the string to PUT statement. The string must be enclosed in quotation marks.

*Example:* In the following program a raw data file *'questfile'* is created using the Data Set *exam.questionset3*. In this program the string to be written to the raw data file is mentioned in the PUT statement.

*data _null_ ;*

    *set exam.questionset3;*

    *file 'c:\sas\questfile';*

*put 'Author is ' author 'The start date is 'startdate : date9.;*

*run;*


**184: Is it possible to skip certain fields while using LIST input?**

**Answer:**

While using LIST input, it is not possible to skip the fields in between. Also, list does not allow re-reading of fields. Fields must be read in order from left to right while using LIST input. Fields must be separated by one blank or any other delimiter.

This page is intentionally left blank

# Chapter 16

# Date and Time Value

**185: While storing dates, does SAS adjusts for daylight saving time?**

**Answer:**

No, SAS does not make adjustments for daylight saving time, but SAS does adjust for leap years but ignores leap seconds.

**186: Explain DATEw. Informat in detail.**

**Answer:**

*DATEw. Informat* reads the date values in either *ddmmmyy* or *ddmmmyyyy* where:

*dd* is an integer value representing day of the month. It can range from 0-31.

*mmm* represents first three letters of a month's name

*yy* or *yyyy* represents the year

*Example: DATE9. Informat* reads the data values in the following
format: *ddmmmyyyy*(24Apr2012).

### 187: What is the least acceptable field width for *TIMEw. Informat?*

**Answer:**

*TIMEw. Informat* requires a least acceptable field width of 5. If any
width less than 5 is specified, an error message gets generated in
the log.

*Example:* This example is to show the use of *TIMEw. Informat*

*TIME5. Informat* reads the data values in *hh*:*mm*(10:20) where:

*hh* represents hour and can range from 00 to 23

*mm* represents minutes and can range from 00 to 59.

### 188: Explain *WORDDATEw.* Format.

**Answer:**

*WORDDATEw.* is a date format which writes the values in '*month
name dd, yyyy*' where:

*dd* represents the day of the month and can range from 1 to 31

*yyyy* represents year

*Example:* In the following example, the values of the variable
'*startdate*' are stored in the following format *month name dd, yyyy*
(April 24, 2012)

*data exam.questionset3;*

   *infile questfile dsd;*

*length author $ 20;*

*input slno 1-3 @5 author  $12. startdate : date9. ;*

*format startdate worddate14.;*

*run;*

### 189: How does YEARCUTOFF= system option affect the 4-digit year values?

**Answer:**

YEARCUTOFF= system option has no effect on the 4-digit year values. 4-digityear values are read correctly. While working with 2-digit year data it is always necessary to check the default value of YEARCUTOFF= system option and change it if necessary.

### 190: Explain *WEEKDATEw.* Format.

**Answer:**

*WEEKDATEw.* is a date format which writes the values in format which displays the day of the week, month, day and year. The general format in which values are written is: '*Day of the week, month name dd, yyyy*' where

*dd* represents the day of the month and can range from 1 to 31

*yyyy* represents year

*Example:* In the following example, the values of the variable '*startdate*' are stored in *day of the week, month name dd, yyyy* (Tue, Apr 24, 2012)

*data exam.questionset3;*

*infile questfile dsd;*

*length author $ 20;*

*input slno 1-3 @5 author  $12. startdate : date9. ;*

*format startdate weekdate17.;*

*run;*

## 191: Explain TIMEw. Informat.

**Answer:**

INFORMATw. is used to read date/time variables from flat files. TIMEw. is used to read time in the format *hh:mm:ss.ss* wherein *hh* represents the hour which can be an integer between 0 to 23, *mm* represents the minute which can be an integer ranging from 0 to 59 and ss.ss represents the seconds with milliseconds which can range from 0.0 to 59.59 again. *ss.ss* is an optional value.

*Example*: In the following program the INFORMAT used (Time11.) reads the values of the variable '*starttime*' in the form *hh:mm:ss.ss*. So a sample value would be 10:50:01.34

*data exam.questionset3;*

*infile questfile dsd;*

*length author $ 20;*

*input slno author & $12. starttime Time11. ;*

*run;*

## 192: How does SAS store date and time and what is the advantage?

**Answer:**

SAS stores date and time as numeric values. SAS date value is counted as number of days from Jan1, 1960 to the given date. When a SAS INFORMAT is used to read a date, SAS converts it into a numeric value. A SAS time value is counted as number of seconds since midnight. The greatest advantage of storing date and time as numeric value is that they can be used in numeric calculations just like any other numeric variable. This feature is not available in most of the programming languages.

This page is intentionally left blank

# Chapter **17**

# Line Pointer Controls

**193: Explain #n line pointer control in SAS.**

**Answer:**

#n specifies the number of line to which you intend to move the pointer control in SAS. Suppose the data which you wish to read has observations spread over different lines, #n pointer helps in reading the records in any order. This has to be mentioned in the input statement.

*Example:* In the following program a Data Set *exam.questionset3* is created from the file specified by *'questfile'*. In the raw data file, a single observation is spread over 4 lines. So, use of #n line pointer enables us to read the *'slno'* first by specifying #4. *'slno'* is in 4th line in the raw data file. Next, we wish to go to first line to read the value of *'author1'*. So, #1 is specified. The value of *'author2'* is in the third line in the raw data file. So, we use #3 to move to 3rd line. Finally, to read the value of *'author3'* which is in the second line, #2 pointer is specified.

*data exam.questionset3;*

  *infile questfile;*

*input #4 slno*

  *#1 author1 $*

  *#3 author2 $*

  *#2 author3 $;*

*run;*


**194: Explain forward slash(/) line pointer control in SAS.**

**Answer:**

Forward slash(/) line pointer is used to specify the location of a line relative to the current line. Forward slash(/) is used to read the records sequentially. This needs to be mentioned in the input statement and it moves the pointer to the next line.

*Example:* In the following program a Data Set *exam.questionset3* is created from the file specified by *'questfile'*. In the raw data file, a single observation is spread over 4 lines. Here the input statement reads the value of *'slno'* from the first line. Then the forward slash operator(/) moves the line pointer to second line .Value of *'author1'* is read from second record and forward slash operator moves the line pointer control to third line. Value of *'author2'* is read and again the / operator moves the pointer to 4th line thereby reading the value of *'author3'*.

*data exam.questionset3;*

  *infile questfile;*

*input slno/*

> *author1 $/*
>
> *author2 $/*
>
> *author3 $;*

*run;*

**195: Is it possible to combine both the line pointer controls (#n and /) in a SAS program to read the data both sequentially and non-sequentially?**

**Answer:**

Yes, it is possible to combine both the line pointer controls (#n and /) in a SAS program to read the data both sequentially and non-sequentially.

*Example:* In the following program a Data Set *exam.questionset3* is created from the file specified by *'questfile'*. In the raw data file, a single observation is spread over 4 lines. Here the input statement reads the value of *'slno'* from the fourth line with the help of #4-line pointer control. Then the #1-line pointer control moves the line pointer to first line and reads the value of *'author1'*. Forward slash operator moves the line pointer control to second line. Value of *'author2'* is read and again the / operator moves the pointer to third line thereby reading the value of *'author3'*.

*data exam.questionset3;*

> *infile questfile;*

*input #4 slno*

> *#1 author1 $/*
>
> *author2 $/*
>
> *author3 $;*

*run;*

**196: While reading a file which contains multiple records per observation, what things need to be considered?**

**Answer:**

SAS uses line pointer controls to read multiple records per observation. The following points needs to be considered while reading:

   a) The input file should contain the same number of records for each observation that is created.

   b) All the observations must be spread over equal number of lines.

   c) A semicolon must be placed after the end of complete input statement.

   d) SAS statements can spread over different lines.

*Example:* In the following program a Data Set *exam.questionset3* is created from the file specified by *'questfile'*. In the raw data file, a single observation is spread over 4 lines. This is applicable for all the observations in the raw data file. Also, the semi-colon is placed at the end of input statement after all the observations are read.

*data exam.questionset3;*

   *infile questfile;*

      *input #4 slno*

         *#1 author1 $/*

         *author2 $/*

         *author3 $;*

*run;*

**197: Explain the significance of REMOVE statement.**

**Answer:**

REMOVE statement is used to delete an observation from a SAS Data Set. It is used with a MODIFY statement.

*Example:* The following program shows an example of REMOVE statement. This deletes an observation from *exam.questionset1* whose value of *'slno'* is equal to 2050.

*data exam.questionset1;*

  *modify exam.questionset1;*

*if slno=2050 then remove;*

*run;*

**198: Explain the trailing (@) line hold specifier.**

**Answer:**

Sometimes the raw data file may contain multiple observations per record. So, while using input statement, we need to hold the current record until each set of data is read and written to Data Set as separate observations. This is accomplished by using line hold specifiers. The Trailing (@) sign holds the record for execution of next input statement.

*Example:* In the following program a Data Set *exam.questionset3* is created from the file specified by *'questfile'*. The file structure is such that each record consists of one serial number and four authors. Here we are planning to create one observation for each author in the new Data Set. So, in the new Data Set each observation is planned to have a serial number and one author. The first input statement reads the value of *'slno'* and holds the record for reading the subsequent values of authors. Since there are four values of authors a *DO loop* is built to read each value of author. So, each observation would have *'slno'* and value of *'author'*.

```
data exam.questionset3;
  infile questfile;
input slno  $ @;
   do i=1 to 4;
   input author & $12. @;
   output;
   end;
run;
```

## 199: Explain double trailing (@@) sign in detail.

### Answer:

Sometimes the raw data file may contain multiple observations per record. So, while using input statement, we need to hold the current record until each set of data is read and written to Data Set as separate observations. This is accomplished by using line hold specifiers. The double trailing (@@) sign holds the record for execution of next input statement, even across iterations of a data step.

*Example:* In the following program a Data Set *exam.questionset3* is created from the file specified by *'questfile'*. The input file structure is such that each record consists of three sets of *'slno'* and *'author'*. Since each record consist of three sets of values, data step must execute 3 times for each record. The input statement reads the value of *'slno'* and *'author'* and holds the current record by using double trailing (@@). The values are written to the program data vector and the control again returns to the top of data step. In the next iteration of data step, next set of values (next values of *'slno'* and *'author'*) are read from the same record.

*data exam.questionset3;*

*infile questfile;*

    *input slno author & $12. @@;*

*run;*


**200: When is a record which is held by double trailing (@@) line hold specifier released?**

**Answer:**

A record which is held by the double trailing sign (@@) is released when one of the following occurs:

    a)   The input pointer moves past the end of the record i.e. the input pointer moves to the next record.

    b)   An input which has no line hold specifier executes. (Example for an input statement without any line hold specifier : input *slno author & $12.;*)


**201: In which situations is double trailing (@@) not allowed?**

**Answer:**

Double trailing (@@) line hold specifier should not be used with @ pointer control, COLUMN input or with MISSOVER option.


**202: When is a record which is held by single trailing (@) line hold specifier released?**

**Answer:**

A record which is held by the single trailing sign (@) is released when the control returns to the top of data step for next iteration. It does not hold the record across iterations of data step.

**203: What will happen in a situation where a record is held by a single trailing (@) sign and another input statement which has a trailing (@) sign executes?**

**Answer:**

Even if during the holding of a record, another input statement with a single trailing(@) executes, there is no impact and the holding effect is still on.

**204: How do you deal with records with varying number of fields while using single trailing sign(@)?**

**Answer:**

While using single trailing sign (@) line hold specifier, if records are having varying number of fields, MISSOVER option is used in the INFILE statement. Here, as the records are having varying number of fields, they are considered as records with missing values at the end of the record.

*Example:* In the following program a Data Set *exam.questionset3* is created from the file specified by *'questfile'*. The file structure is such that first record is having 3 values (*slno, author, author*) and second record has two values (*slno, author*). Here the input statement reads the value of *'slno'* and first value of *'author'*. The trailing sign (@) holds the record so that subsequent values of *author* can be read. MISSOVER option prevents reading past the end of the record.

*data exam.questionset3;*

   *infile questfile missover;*

*input slno author& $12. @;*

*run;*

## 205: Explain STOPOVER option in detail.

**Answer:**

External files may contain raw data which may contain variable length record or records having missing values. While reading such data, SAS may not be able to find the values for all the variables specified in the input statement. When no option is used in the INFILE statement, SAS goes to next record to fetch the values of current observation. This may lead to inaccurate data in the output Data Set. STOPOVER is one of the options which helps to control how SAS reads past the end of the line. STOPOVER option causes SAS to stop processing when it does not find the values for all the variables specified in the input statement. When sufficient values for all the variables are not there, use of this option causes the value of error variable (_ERROR_) to be set to 1.

*Example:* In the following program a Data Set *exam.questionset3* is created from the file specified by *'questfile'*. While reading the raw data file, if any record contains no values for either *'slno'* or *'author'* the use of STOPOVER function causes the data step to stop processing.

*data exam.questionset3;*

  *infile questfile stopover;*

    *input slno author & $12.;*

*run;*

## 206: While reading the data from an external file, which option is used to determine the end of the file condition?

**Answer:**

It is possible to determine if the current record is the last record in the external file by using END= option in the INFILE statement.

Like other automatic variables, the value of END= variable is not written to the Data Set.

*Example:* In the following program a Data Set *exam.questionset3* is created from the file specified by *'questfile'*. In this example end= option creates a temporary variable *last*. The variable is numeric and the value changes to 1 when the end of the file is reached.

*data exam.questionset3;*

   *infile questfile end=last;*

      *input slno author & $12.;*

   *if last then output;*

*run;*

**207: Explain FLOWOVER option in detail.**

**Answer:**

External files may contain raw data which may contain variable length records or records having missing values. While reading such data, SAS may not be able to find the values for all the variables specified in the input statement. FLOWOVER option is the default behaviour of input statement. When SAS is not able to find the values of all variables in the current record, it moves to the next record and attempts to find the values to assign to the rest of the variable names in the input statement.

*Example:* In the following program a Data Set *exam.questionset3* is created from the file specified by *questfile*. While reading the raw data file, if any record contains no values for either *slno* or *author* the use of FLOWOVER function causes the data step to move to next record and attempt to find the value for all the variables.

*data exam.questionset3;*

   *infile questfile flowover;*

*input slno author& $12.;*

*run;*

## 208: Explain TRUNCOVER option in detail.

**Answer:**

TRUNCOVER is an INFILE option which enables the data step to assign a raw data value to a variable even if it is shorter than what is expected by the input statement. If the data step is unable to find the values for the variable at the end of input record, then SAS assigns missing value to that variable.

*Example:* In the following program a Data Set *exam.questionset3* is created from the file specified by *'questfile'*. In this example even though the length of the variable *'setnumber'* is expected to be 12 by the input statement, the use of TRUNCOVER statement causes the values which are shorter than 12 also to be read.

*data exam.questionset3;*

  *infile questfilet runcover;*

    *input setnumber 12.;*

*run;*

## 209: Explain the LINESIZE option.

**Answer:**

LINESIZE is an INFILE option which is used to specify the record length which is available to the input statement. The value of LINESIZE can range from 1 to 32,767. If input statement attempts to read past the value which is specified by the LINESIZE= option, then the output depends on the other options specified in the INFILE statement (FLOWOVER, MISSOVER, STOPOVER or

TRUNCOVER). FLOWOVER is the default.

*Example:* In the following program a Data Set *exam.questionset3* is created from the file specified by *'questfile'*. The LINESIZE is limited to 72.

*data exam.questionset3;*

*infile questfile linesize=72 flowover;*

*input setnumber 12.;*

*run;*

**210: Is it possible to create more than one Data Set in a single data step?**

**Answer:**

Yes, it is possible to create more than one Data Set using a single data step. This can be achieved by mentioning the names of Data Sets to be created in the data statement.

*Example:* In the following simple program three Data Sets are created: *exam.questionset3, exam.questionset4* and *exam.questionset5* by reading the input Data Set *exam.questionset2.*

*data exam.questionset3 exam.questionset4 exam.questionset5;*

*set exam.questionset2;*

*run;*

**211: How do you rename one or more Data Sets in the same library?**

**Answer:**

It is possible to rename one or more Data Sets in the same library using CHANGE statement in Data Sets procedure.

*Example:* The following example renames two Data Sets in the SAS data library *'exam'*. The following program starts the Data Sets procedure and changes the name of the Data Set *questionset1* to *set1* and the name of the Data Set *questionset2* to *set2*. As it is processed, a statement is written to the log stating that the Data Sets have been renamed.

*proc datasets library=exam;*

   *change questionset1=set1 questionset2=set2;*

*quit;*

**212: How do you modify a label which was permanently assigned in a data step previously?**

**Answer:**

It is possible to modify a label which was previously assigned in a data step by using MODIFY statement and its subordinate LABEL statement in Data Sets procedure.

*Example:* The following program starts the Data Set procedure and specifies the input library to be *'exam'*. MODIFY statement specifies the name of the Data Set. The variable *'author'* gets new label *'technical author'*.

*proc datasets library=exam;*

*modify questionset1;*

   *label author='technical author';*

*quit;*

**213: Is it possible to rename variables in a Data Set using Data Sets procedure?**

**Answer:**

It is possible to rename variables of a Data Set by using MODIFY statement and its subordinate RENAME statement in Data Sets procedure.

*Example:* The following program starts the Data Set procedure and specifies the input library to be *'exam'*. MODIFY statement specifies the name of the Data Set whose variable needs to be renamed. The variable *'author1'* gets renamed to *'techauthor1'*.

*proc datasets library=exam;*

*modify questionset1;*

   *rename author1=techauthor1;*

*quit;*

### 214: Is it possible to copy the Data Sets from one library to another using programming statements?

**Answer:**

It is possible to copy specific Data Sets from one library to another by using copy statement in Data Sets procedure.

*Example:* The following program starts the Data Set procedure and specifies the input library to be *'exam'*. COPY statement specifies the name of the library from which Data Set is to be copied in the IN= option and also specifies the name of the library to which the Data Set is to be copied in OUT= option. SELECT statement specifies the name of the Data Set. Here the Data Set *'questionset1'* is to be copied from *'exam'* library to *'finalexam'* library.

*proc datasets;*

   *copy in=exam out=finalexam;*

      *select questionset1;*

*quit;*

**215: Explain the significance of EXCLUDE statement while using COPY statement.**

**Answer:**

EXCLUDE statement is used with COPY statement when you want to copy an entire library except few Data Sets.

*Example:* The following program starts the Data Set procedure and specifies the input library to be *'exam'*. COPY statement specifies the name of the name of the library from which files are copied in the IN = option and specifies the name of the library to which the files are to be copied in OUT = option. EXCLUDE statement specifies the name of the Data Set which needs to be excluded. Here all the files except Data Set *questionset1* is to be copied from *'exam'* library to *'finalexam'* library.

*proc datasets;*

   *copy in=exam out=finalexam;*

      *exclude questionset1;*

*quit;*

This page is intentionally left blank

# **HR** Interview Questions

Review these typical interview questions and think about how you would answer them. Read the answers listed; you will find best possible answers along with strategies and suggestions

## 1: How would you handle a negative co-worker?

**Answer:**

Everyone has to deal with negative co-workers – and the single best way to do so is to remain positive. You may try to build a relationship with the co-worker or relate to them in some way, but even if your efforts are met with a cold shoulder, you must retain your positive attitude. Above all, stress that you would never allow a co-worker's negativity to impact your own work or productivity.

## 2: What would you do if you witnessed a co-worker surfing the web, reading a book, etc, wasting company time?

**Answer:**

The interviewer will want to see that you realize how detrimental it is for employees to waste company time, and that it is not something you take lightly. Explain the way you would adhere to company policy, whether that includes talking to the co-worker yourself, reporting the behavior straight to a supervisor, or talking to someone in HR.

## 3: How do you handle competition among yourself and other employees?

**Answer:**

Healthy competition can be a great thing, and it is best to stay focused on the positive aspects of this here. Don't bring up conflict among yourself and other co-workers, and instead focus on the motivation to keep up with the great work of others, and the ways in which co-workers may be a great support network in helping to push you to new successes.

## 4: When is it okay to socialize with co-workers?

**Answer:**

This question has two extreme answers (all the time, or never), and your interviewer, in most cases, will want to see that you fall somewhere in the middle. It's important to establish solid relationships with your co-workers, but never at the expense of getting work done. Ideally, relationship-building can happen with exercises of teamwork and special projects, as well as in the break room.

## 5: Tell me about a time when a major change was made at your last job, and how you handled it.

**Answer:**

Provide a set-up for the situation including the old system, what the change was, how it was implemented, and the results of the change, and include how you felt about each step of the way. Be sure that your initial thoughts on the old system are neutral, and that your excitement level grows with each step of the new change, as an interviewer will be pleased to see your adaptability.

## 6: When delegating tasks, how do you choose which tasks go to which team members?

**Answer:**

The interviewer is looking to gain insight into your thought process with this question, so be sure to offer thorough reasoning behind your choice. Explain that you delegate tasks based on each individual's personal strengths, or that you look at how many other projects each person is working on at the time, in order to create the best fit possible.

**7: Tell me about a time when you had to stand up for something you believed strongly about to co-workers or a supervisor.**

**Answer:**

While it may be difficult to explain a situation of conflict to an interviewer, this is a great opportunity to display your passions and convictions, and your dedication to your beliefs. Explain not just the situation to the interviewer, but also elaborate on why it was so important to you to stand up for the issue, and how your co-worker or supervisor responded to you afterward – were they more respectful? Unreceptive? Open-minded? Apologetic?

**8: Tell me about a time when you helped someone finish their work, even though it wasn't "your job."**

**Answer:**

Though you may be frustrated when required to pick up someone else's slack, it's important that you remain positive about lending a hand. The interviewer will be looking to see if you're a team player, and by helping someone else finish a task that he or she couldn't manage alone, you show both your willingness to help the team succeed, and your own competence.

**9: What are the challenges of working on a team? How do you handle this?**

**Answer:**

There are many obvious challenges to working on a team, such as handling different perspectives, navigating individual schedules, or accommodating difficult workers. It's best to focus on one challenge, such as individual team members missing deadlines or failing to keep commitments, and then offer a solution that clearly addresses the problem. For example, you could organize weekly status meetings for your team to discuss progress or assign shorter deadlines in order to keep the long-term deadline on schedule.

### 10: Do you value diversity in the workplace?

**Answer:**

Diversity is important in the workplace in order to foster an environment that is accepting, equalizing, and full of different perspectives and backgrounds. Be sure to show your awareness of these issues and stress the importance of learning from others' experiences.

### 11: How would you handle a situation in which a co-worker was not accepting of someone else's diversity?

Answer:

Explain that it is important to adhere to company policies regarding diversity, and that you would talk to the relevant supervisors or management team. When it is appropriate, it could also be best to talk to the co-worker in question about the benefits of alternate perspectives – if you can handle the situation yourself, it's best not to bring resolvable issues to management.

### 12: Are you rewarded more from working on a team, or accomplishing a task on your own?

**Answer:**

It's best to show a balance between these two aspects – your employer wants to see that you're comfortable working on your own, and that you can complete tasks efficiently and well without assistance. However, it's also important for your employer to see that you can be a team player, and that you understand the value that multiple perspectives and efforts can bring to a project.

### 13: Tell me about a time when you didn't meet a deadline.

**Answer:**

Ideally, this hasn't happened – but if it has, make sure you use a minor example to illustrate the situation, emphasize how long ago it happened, and be sure that you did as much as you could to ensure that the deadline was met. Additionally, be sure to include what you learned about managing time better or prioritizing tasks in order to meet all future deadlines.

### 14: How do you eliminate distractions while working?

**Answer:**

With the increase of technology and the ease of communication, new distractions arise every day. Your interviewer will want to see that you are still able to focus on work, and that your productivity has not been affected, by an example showing a routine you employ in order to stay on task.

### 15: Tell me about a time when you worked in a position with a weekly or monthly quota to meet. How often were you successful?

**Answer:**

Your numbers will speak for themselves, and you must answer this question honestly. If you were regularly met your quotas, be sure to highlight this in a confident manner and don't be shy in pointing out your strengths in this area. If your statistics are less than stellar, try to point out trends in which they increased toward the end of your employment, and show reflection as to ways you can improve in the future.

**16: Tell me about a time when you met a tough deadline, and how you were able to complete it.**

**Answer:**

Explain how you were able to prioritize tasks, or to delegate portions of an assignments to other team members, in order to deal with a tough deadline. It may be beneficial to specify why the deadline was tough – make sure it's clear that it was not a result of procrastination on your part. Finally, explain how you were able to successfully meet the deadline, and what it took to get there in the end.

**17: How do you stay organized when you have multiple projects on your plate?**

**Answer:**

The interviewer will be looking to see that you can manage your time and work well – and being able to handle multiple projects at once, and still giving each the attention it deserves, is a great mark of a worker's competence and efficiency. Go through a typical process of goal-setting and prioritizing, and explain the steps of these to the interviewer, so he or she can see how well you manage time.

**18: How much time during your work day do you spend on "auto-pilot?"**

**Answer:**

While you may wonder if the employer is looking to see how

efficient you are with this question (for example, so good at your job that you don't have to think about it), but in almost every case, the employer wants to see that you're constantly thinking, analyzing, and processing what's going on in the workplace. Even if things are running smoothly, there's usually an opportunity somewhere to make things more efficient or to increase sales or productivity. Stress your dedication to ongoing development and convey that being on "auto-pilot" is not conducive to that type of success.

### 19: How do you handle deadlines?

**Answer:**

The most important part of handling tough deadlines is to prioritize tasks and set goals for completion, as well as to delegate or eliminate unnecessary work. Lead the interviewer through a general scenario and display your competency through your ability to organize and set priorities, and most importantly, remain calm.

### 20: Tell me about your personal problem-solving process.

**Answer:**

Your personal problem-solving process should include outlining the problem, coming up with possible ways to fix the problem, and setting a clear action plan that leads to resolution. Keep your answer brief and organized, and explain the steps in a concise, calm manner that shows you are level-headed even under stress.

### 21: What sort of things at work can make you stressed?

**Answer:**

As it's best to stay away from negatives, keep this answer brief and simple. While answering that nothing at work makes you stressed will not be very believable to the interviewer, keep your answer to one generic principle such as when members of a team don't keep their commitments, and then focus on a solution you generally employ to tackle that stress, such as having weekly status meetings or intermittent deadlines along the course of a project.

**22: What do you look like when you are stressed about something? How do you solve it?**

**Answer:**

This is a trick question – your interviewer wants to hear that you don't look any different when you're stressed, and that you don't allow negative emotions to interfere with your productivity. As far as how you solve your stress, it's best if you have a simple solution mastered, such as simply taking deep breaths and counting to 10 to bring yourself back to the task at hand.

**23: Can you multi-task?**

**Answer:**

Some people can, and some people can't. The most important part of multi-tasking is to keep a clear head at all times about what needs to be done, and what priority each task falls under. Explain how you evaluate tasks to determine priority, and how you manage your time in order to ensure that all are completed efficiently.

## 24: How many hours per week do you work?

**Answer:**

Many people get tricked by this question, thinking that answering more hours is better – however, this may cause an employer to wonder why you have to work so many hours in order to get the work done that other people can do in a shorter amount of time. Give a fair estimate of hours that it should take you to complete a job and explain that you are also willing to work extra whenever needed.

## 25: How many times per day do you check your email?

**Answer:**

While an employer wants to see that you are plugged into modern technology, it is also important that the number of times you check your email per day is relatively low – perhaps two to three times per day (dependent on the specific field you're in). Checking email is often a great distraction in the workplace, and while it is important to remain connected, much correspondence can simply be handled together in the morning and afternoon.

## 26: Tell me about a time when you worked additional hours to finish a project.

**Answer:**

It's important for your employer to see that you are dedicated to your work, and willing to put in extra hours when required or when a job calls for it. However, be careful when explaining why you were called to work additional hours – for instance, did you have to stay late because you set goals poorly earlier in the process? Or on a more positive note, were you working additional hours because a client requested for a deadline to be moved up on short notice? Stress your competence and willingness to give 110% every time.

**27: Tell me about a time when your performance exceeded the duties and requirements of your job.**

**Answer:**

If you're a great candidate for the position, this should be an easy question to answer – choose a time when you truly went above and beyond the call of duty and put in additional work or voluntarily took on new responsibilities. Remain humble, and express gratitude for the learning opportunity, as well as confidence in your ability to give a repeat performance.

**28: What is your driving attitude about work?**

**Answer:**

There are many possible good answers to this question, and the interviewer primarily wants to see that you have a great passion for the job and that you will remain motivated in your career if hired. Some specific driving forces behind your success may include hard work, opportunity, growth potential, or success.

**29: Do you take work home with you?**

**Answer:**

It is important to first clarify that you are always willing to take work home when necessary, but you want to emphasize as well that it has not been an issue for you in the past. Highlight skills such as time management, goal-setting, and multi-tasking, which can all ensure that work is completed at work.

## 30: Describe a typical work day to me.

**Answer:**

There are several important components in your typical work day, and an interviewer may derive meaning from any or all of them, as well as from your ability to systematically lead him or her through the day. Start at the beginning of your day and proceed chronologically, making sure to emphasize steady productivity, time for review, goal-setting, and prioritizing, as well as some additional time to account for unexpected things that may arise.

## 31: Tell me about a time when you went out of your way at your previous job.

**Answer:**

Here it is best to use a specific example of the situation that required you to go out of your way, what your specific position would have required that you did, and how you went above that. Use concrete details, and be sure to include the results, as well as reflection on what you learned in the process.

## 32: Are you open to receiving feedback and criticisms on your job performance, and adjusting as necessary?

**Answer:**

This question has a pretty clear answer – yes – but you'll need to display a knowledge as to why this is important. Receiving feedback and criticism is one thing, but the most important part of that process is to then implement it into your daily work. Keep a good attitude, and express that you always appreciate constructive feedback.

**33: What inspires you?**

**Answer:**

You may find inspiration in nature, reading success stories, or mastering a difficult task, but it's important that your inspiration is positively-based and that you're able to listen and tune into it when it appears. Keep this answer generally based in the professional world, but where applicable, it may stretch a bit into creative exercises in your personal life that, in turn, help you in achieving career objectives.

**34: How do you inspire others?**

**Answer:**

This may be a difficult question, as it is often hard to discern the effects of inspiration in others. Instead of offering a specific example of a time when you inspired someone, focus on general principles such as leading by example that you employ in your professional life. If possible, relate this to a quality that someone who inspired you possessed, and discuss the way you have modified or modeled it in your own work.

**35: How do you make decisions?**

**Answer:**

This is a great opportunity for you to wow your interviewer with your decisiveness, confidence, and organizational skills. Make sure that you outline a process for decision-making, and that you stress the importance of weighing your options, as well as in trusting intuition. If you answer this question skilfully and with ease, your interviewer will trust in your capability as a worker.

## 36: What are the most difficult decisions for you to make?

**Answer:**

Explain your relationship to decision-making, and a general synopsis of the process you take in making choices. If there is a particular type of decision that you often struggle with, such as those that involve other people, make sure to explain why that type of decision is tough for you, and how you are currently engaged in improving your skills.

## 37: When making a tough decision, how do you gather information?

**Answer:**

If you're making a tough choice, it's best to gather information from as many sources as possible. Lead the interviewer through your process of taking information from people in different areas, starting first with advice from experts in your field, feedback from co-workers or other clients, and by looking analytically at your own past experiences.

## 38: Tell me about a decision you made that did not turn out well.

**Answer:**

Honesty and transparency are great values that your interviewer will appreciate – outline the choice you made, why you made it, the results of your poor decision – and finally (and most importantly!) what you learned from the decision. Give the interviewer reason to trust that you wouldn't make a decision like that again in the future.

## 39: Are you able to make decisions quickly?

**Answer:**

You may be able to make decisions quickly but be sure to communicate your skill in making sound, thorough decisions as well. Discuss the importance of making a decision quickly, and how you do so, as well as the necessity for each decision to first be well-informed.

## 40: Ten years ago, what were your career goals?

**Answer:**

In reflecting back to what your career goals were ten years ago, it's important to show the ways in which you've made progress in that time. Draw distinct links between specific objectives that you've achieved and speak candidly about how it felt to reach those goals. Remain positive, upbeat, and growth-oriented, even if you haven't yet achieved all of the goals you set out to reach.

## 41: Tell me about a weakness you used to have, and how you changed it.

**Answer:**

Choose a non-professional weakness that you used to have and outline the process you went through in order to grow past it. Explain the weakness itself, why it was problematic, the action steps you planned, how you achieved them, and the end result.

## 42: Tell me about your goal-setting process.

**Answer:**

When describing your goal-setting process, clearly outline the way that you create an outline for yourself. It may be helpful to offer an example of a particular goal you've set in the past and use this as a starting point to guide the way you created action steps, check-in points, and how the goal was eventually achieved.

## 43: Tell me about a time when you solved a problem by creating actionable steps to follow.

**Answer:**

This question will help the interviewer to see how you talented you are in outlining, problem resolution, and goal-setting. Explain thoroughly the procedure of outlining the problem, establishing steps to take, and then how you followed the steps (such as through check-in points along the way, or intermediary goals).

## 44: Where do you see yourself five years from now?

**Answer:**

Have some idea of where you would like to have advanced to in the position you're applying for, over the next several years. Make sure that your future plans line up with you still working for the company and stay positive about potential advancement. Focus on future opportunities, and what you're looking forward to – but make sure your reasons for advancement are admirable, such as greater experience and the chance to learn, rather than simply being out for a higher salary.

## 45: When in a position, do you look for opportunities to promote?

**Answer:**

There's a fine balance in this question – you want to show the interviewer that you have initiative and motivation to advance in your career, but not at the expense of appearing opportunistic or selfishly-motivated. Explain that you are always open to growth opportunities, and very willing to take on new responsibilities as your career advances.

### 46: On a scale of 1 to 10, how successful has your life been?

**Answer:**

Though you may still have a long list of goals to achieve, it's important to keep this answer positively-focused. Choose a high number between 7 and 9 and explain that you feel your life has been largely successful and satisfactory as a result of several specific achievements or experiences. Don't go as high as a 10, as the interviewer may not believe your response or in your ability to reason critically.

### 47: What is your greatest goal in life?

**Answer:**

It's okay for this answer to stray a bit into your personal life, but best if you can keep it professionally-focused. While specific goals are great, if your personal goal doesn't match up exactly with one of the company's objectives, you're better off keeping your goal a little more generic and encompassing, such as "success in my career" or "leading a happy and fulfilling life." Keep your answer brief, and show a decisive nature – most importantly, make it clear that you've already thought about this question and know what you want.

**48: Tell me about a time when you set a goal in your personal life and achieved it.**

**Answer:**

The interviewer can see that you excel at setting goals in your professional life, but he or she also wants to know that you are consistent in your life and capable of setting goals outside of the office as well. Use an example such as making a goal to eat more healthily or to drink more water and discuss what steps you outlined to achieve your goal, the process of taking action, and the final results as well.

**49: What is your greatest goal in your career?**

**Answer:**

Have a very specific goal of something you want to achieve in your career in mind and be sure that it's something the position clearly puts you in line to accomplish. Offer the goal as well as your plans to get there and emphasize clear ways in which this position will be an opportunity to work toward the goal.

**50: Tell me about a time when you achieved a goal.**

**Answer:**

Start out with how you set the goal, and why you chose it. Then, take the interviewer through the process of outlining the goal, taking steps to achieve it, the outcome, and finally, how you felt after achieving it or recognition you received. The most important part of this question includes the planning and implementation of strategies, so focus most of your time on explaining these aspects. However, the preliminary decisions and end results are also important, so make sure to include them as well.

**51: What areas of your work would you still like to improve in? What are your plans to do this?**

**Answer:**

While you may not want the interviewer to focus on things you could improve on, it's important to be self-aware of your own growth opportunities. More importantly, you can impress an interviewer by having specific goals and actions outlined in order to facilitate your growth, even if your area of improvement is something as simple as increasing sales or finding new ways to create greater efficiency.

**52: What is customer service?**

**Answer:**

Customer service can be many things – and the most important consideration in this question is that you have a creative answer. Demonstrate your ability to think outside the box by offering a confident answer that goes past a basic definition, and that shows you have truly considered your own individual view of what it means to take care of your customers. The thoughtful consideration you hold for customers will speak for itself.

**53: Tell me about a time when you went out of your way for a customer.**

**Answer:**

It's important that you offer an example of a time you truly went out of your way – be careful not to confuse something that felt like a big effort on your part, with something your employer would expect you to do anyway. Offer an example of the customer's problems, what you did to solve it, and the way the customer responded after you took care of the situation.

### 54: How do you gain confidence from customers?

Answer:

This is a very open-ended question that allows you to show your customer service skills to the interviewer. There are many possible answers, and it is best to choose something that you've had great experience with, such as "by handling situations with transparency," "offering rewards," or "focusing on great communication." Offer specific examples of successes you've had.

### 55: Tell me about a time when a customer was upset or agitated – how did you handle the situation?

Answer:

Similarly to handling a dispute with another employee, the most important part to answering this question is to first set up the scenario, offer a step-by-step guide to your particular conflict resolution style, and end by describing the way the conflict was resolved. Be sure that in answering questions about your own conflict resolution style, that you emphasize the importance of open communication and understanding from both parties, as well as a willingness to reach a compromise or other solution.

### 56: When can you make an exception for a customer?

Answer:

Exceptions for customers can generally be made when in accordance with company policy or when directed by a supervisor. Display an understanding of the types of situations in which an exception should be considered, such as when a customer has endured a particular hardship, had a complication with an order, or at a request.

### 57: What would you do in a situation where you were needed by both a customer and your boss?

**Answer:**

While both your customer and your boss have different needs of you and are very important to your success as a worker, it is always best to try to attend to your customer first – however, the key is explaining to your boss why you are needed urgently by the customer, and then to assure your boss that you will attend to his or her needs as soon as possible (unless it's absolutely an urgent matter).

### 58: What is the most important aspect of customer service?

**Answer:**

While many people would simply state that customer satisfaction is the most important aspect of customer service, it's important to be able to elaborate on other important techniques in customer service situations. Explain why customer service is such a key part of business and be sure to expand on the aspect that you deem to be the most important in a way that is reasoned and well-thought out.

### 59: Is it best to create low or high expectations for a customer?

**Answer:**

You may answer this question either way (after, of course, determining that the company does not have a clear opinion on the matter). However, no matter which way you answer the question, you must display a thorough thought process, and very clear reasoning for the option you chose. Offer pros and cons of each, and include the ultimate point that tips the scale in favor of your chosen answer.

### 60: Why did you choose your college major?

**Answer:**

It's important to display interest in your work, and if your major is related to your current field, it will be simple for you to relate the two. Perhaps you even knew while in college that you wanted to do a job similar to this position, and so you chose the major so as to receive the education and training you needed to succeed. If your major doesn't relate clearly, it's still important to express a sense of passion for your choice, and to specify the importance of pursuing something that matters to you – which is how you made the decision to come to your current career field instead.

### 61: Tell me about your college experience.

**Answer:**

It's best to keep this answer positive – don't focus on parties, pizza, or procrastinating. Instead, offer a general summary of the benefits you received in college, followed by an anecdote of a favorite professor or course that opened up your way of thinking about the field you're in. This is a great opportunity for you to show your passion for your career, make sure to answer enthusiastically and confidently.

## 62: What is the most unique thing about yourself that you would bring to this position?

**Answer:**

This question is often asked as a close to an interview, and it gives you a final chance to highlight your best qualities to the employer. Treat the question like a sort of review, and explain why your specific mix of education, experience, and passions will be the ideal combination for the employer. Remain confident but humble and keep your answer to about two minutes.

## 63: How did your last job stand up to your previous expectations of it?

**Answer:**

While it's okay to discuss what you learned if you expected too much out of a previous job, it's best to keep this question away from negative statements or portrayals. Focus your answer around what your previous job did hold that you had expected, and how much you enjoyed those aspects of the position.

## 64: How did you become interested in this field?

**Answer:**

This is the chance for you to show your passion for your career – and the interviewer will be assured that you are a great candidate if it's obvious that you enjoy your job. You can include a brief anecdote here in order to make your interest personal but be sure that it is brief. Offer specific names of mentors or professors who aided in your discovery and make it clear that you love what you do.

## 65: What was the greatest thing you learned while in school?

**Answer:**

By offering a lesson you learned outside of the classroom, you can show the interviewer your capacity for creativity, learning, and reflection. The practical lessons you learned in the classroom are certainly invaluable in their own right and may pertain closely to the position but showing the mastery of a concept that you had to learn on your own will highlight your growth potential.

## 66: Tell me about a time when you had to learn a different skill set for a new position.

**Answer:**

Use a specific example to describe what you had to learn and how you set about outlining goals and tasks for yourself. It's important to show that you mastered the skill largely from your dedication to learning it, and because of the systematic approach you took to developing and honing your individual education. Additionally, draw connections between the skill you learned and the new position, and show how well prepared you are for the job.

## 67: Tell me about a person who has been a great influence in your career.

**Answer:**

It's important to make this answer easy to relate to – your story should remind the interviewer of the person who was most influential in his or her own career. Explain what you learned from this person and why they inspired you, and how you hope to model them later in your career with future successes.

## 68: What would this person tell me about you?

**Answer:**

Most importantly, if this person is one of your references –they had better know who you are! There are all too many horror stories of professors or past employers being called for a reference, and not being able to recall when they knew you or why you were remarkable, which doesn't send a very positive message to potential employers. This person should remember you as being enthusiastic, passionate, and motivated to learn and succeed.

## 69: What is the most productive time of day for you?

**Answer:**

This is a trick question – you should be equally productive all day! While it's normal to become extra motivated for certain projects, and also true that some tasks will require additional work, be sure to emphasize to the interviewer that working diligently throughout the entirety of the day comes naturally to you.

## 70: What was the most responsibility you were given at your previous job?

**Answer:**

This question provides you with an opportunity to elaborate on responsibilities that may or may not be on your resume. For instance, your resume may not have allowed room to discuss individual projects you worked on that were really outside the scope of your job responsibilities, but you can tell the interviewer here about the additional work you did and how it translated into new skills and a richer career experience for you.

## 71: Do you believe you were compensated fairly at your last job?

**Answer:**

Remember to stay positive, and to avoid making negative comments about your previous employer. If you were not compensated fairly, simply state that you believe your qualities and experience were outside the compensation limitations of the old job, and that you're looking forward to an opportunity that is more in line with the place you're at in your career.

## 72: Tell me about a time when you received feedback on your work and enacted it.

**Answer:**

Try to give an example of feedback your received early in your career, and the steps you took to incorporate it with your work. The most important part of this question is to display the way you learned from the feedback, as well as your willingness to accept suggestions from your superiors. Be sure to offer reflection and understanding of how the feedback helped your work to improve.

## 73: Tell me about a time when you received feedback on your work that you did not agree with, or thought was unfair. How did you handle it?

**Answer:**

When explaining that you did not agree with particular feedback or felt it was unfair, you'll need to justify tactfully why the feedback was inaccurate. Then, explain how you communicated directly with the person who offered the feedback, and, most importantly, how you listened to their response, analyzed it, and then came to a mutual agreement.

## 74: What was your favorite job, and why?

**Answer:**

It's best if your favorite job relates to the position you're currently applying for, as you can then easily draw connections between why you enjoyed that job and why you are interested in the current position. Additionally, it is extremely important to explain why you've qualified the particular job as your favorite, and what aspects of it you would look for in another job, so that the interviewer can determine whether or not you are a good fit.

## 75: Tell me about an opportunity that your last position did not allow you to achieve.

**Answer:**

Stay focused on the positive and be understanding of the limitations of your previous position. Give a specific example of a goal or career objective that you were not able to achieve, but rather than expressing disappointment over the missed opportunity, discuss the ways you're looking forward to the chance to grow in a new position.

## 76: Tell me about the worst boss you ever had.

**Answer:**

It's important to keep this answer brief, and positively focused. While you may offer a couple of short, critical assessments of your boss, focus on the things you learned from working with such an individual, and remain sympathetic to challenges the boss may have faced.

# INDEX

## Base SAS Interview Questions

### Basics

1: Explain SAS and its functions.

2: What are the different types of output produced by SAS?

3: You might be already familiar with the Data Set. What is the descriptor portion of the Data Set?

4: Which parameters describe a variable in SAS?

5: How does SAS recognise the end of a step and execute the previous step?

6: How can a permanent SAS Data Set be referenced?

7: What is the default length of numeric variables?

### Referencing Files

8: How do you refer an external file in SAS?

9: Explain the GSUBMIT Command.

10: How do you verify after assigning a LIBREF?

11: What is the purpose of a SAS engine?

12: Describe some ways to view the contents of SAS Data Set.

13: Which option is used to list the variables in creation order or order of logical position while viewing the Data Set with PROC CONTENTS?

14: How do you modify SAS system options like page number, time etc?

15: How SAS handles two-digit year values?

16: Suppose your Data Set *exam.questionset2* contains 20 observations. How do you print only the last 11 observations?

17: Suppose your Data Set *exam.questionset2* contains 20 observations. How do you print the observations from 12-17?

18:  Describe the SOURCE system option used in SAS.

19:  Describe the REPLACE option in detail.

## SAS Programs

20:  What is the purpose of adding @@ in an input statement after the variable?

21:  Explain the difference between FORMAT and INFORMAT.

22:  How is table lookup done in SAS?

23:  What is the function of INCLUDE command in SAS?

24:  What are the two categories of error commonly encountered in SAS?

25:  Suppose after submitting a SAS program you see the statement 'Data step running' at the top of active window. What does that indicate and how do you resolve the issue?

26:  How do you specify comments in SAS?

27:  How do you invoke the debugger in SAS?

## Reports – List and Summary

28:  What's the difference between the Print and Report commands?

29:  Explain the REPORT Procedure.

30:  How do you select the variables and control the order in which they appear while creating a list report?

31:  How to remove the column containing observation number while creating a list report?

32:  What is the output of PROC PRINT?

33:  How do you cancel a title statement?

34:  Suppose you are having a Data Set *exam.questionset2*.The Data Set contains a column date. You have to assign a format (*mmddyy*8.) temporarily to the date column so that it appears in the formatted way in the output. How do you do that?

35:  How do you assign a permanent label in SAS?

36:  While creating a list report with PROC REPORT how do you select the variables and order them?

37: Which option is used with PROC REPORT statement to underline all column headings and space between them?

38: What is the purpose of using order option in the define statement while using PROC REPORT?

39: Which variables are used to calculate statistics in PROC REPORT?

## SAS Data Sets

40: What is the difference between DATALINES and CARDS statements?

41: How do you create a permanent data step?

42: What is the function of INFILE statement?

43: Which is the ideal situation for using COLUMN input?

44: How do you read the data lines entered directly into the program?

45: What is the purpose of using the keyword _NULL_ in the data statement?

46: What is the purpose of PUT statement?

47: Which parameters are to be mentioned in the input statement while using COLUMN input?

48: Usage of programming statement is one common way of creating a SAS Data Set from raw data file. What is the other way of creating SAS Data Set from a raw data file?

49: What is the scope of a FILENAME statement?

50: What is the significance of SET statement in SAS?

51: Is it possible to use date constants to assign dates in ASSIGNMENT statements?

## Data Step

52: Explain the CONTENTS procedure.

53: How can you optimally handle large Data Sets using SAS?

54: Explain the compilation phase of data step in detail.

55: When is an input buffer created?

56: Explain the automatic variable _ERROR_.

57: Explain the significance of _N_.

58: How do you limit the number of observations that are read during the data step?

## Formats

59: What is the maximum length of label?

60: Explain the function of the keyword FMTLIB.

61: How is VALUE statement used to create formats?

62: Which keyword is used in the value statement to label the missing value?

## Statistics

63: Explain Factor Analysis.

64: Explain PROC SUMMARY.

65: Which is the ideal procedure to use for calculating the statistics for continuous numeric variables?

66: What are the default statistics produced by the MEANS procedure?

67: Suppose you had a Data Setexam.set1 for which you wish to calculate the median of all numeric variables. How do you use the programming statements?

68: Which option is used in the PROC MEANS statement to limit the number of decimal places?

69: How do you specify variables in PROC MEANS statement?

70: Which statistics are generated for class variables in MEANS procedure?

71: How can you prevent the default report creation in PROC MEANS?

72: What is the default output produced by PROC FREQ?

73: How do you specify variables to be processed by PROC FREQ?

74: Explain the significance of NOCUM option.

75: What are the criteria for the data to be used for BY group processing?

76: What is the difference between the default output produced by PROC MEANS and PROC SUMMARY?

77: What are the default values produced when PROC FREQ is used for producing crosstabulations?

78: Which keyword is used with PROC MEANS to compute standard deviation?

79: How will you produce a report with PROC SUMMARY?

80: Which types of values are ideal for frequency distribution?

## Outputs

81: Could you list some ODS destinations which are currently supported?

82: How do you use the ODS statement to open LISTING destination?

83: Which ODS destination is open by default?

84: Which keyword is used in ODS statements to close all the open destinations at once?

85: How does ODS handle the output?

86: How do you write the ODS statements to create a simple HTML output?

87: Which option is used in ODS HTML statement to specify the location of storing the output?

## Variables

88: How does the SUM statement deal with the missing values?

89: How does an ASSIGNMENT statement deal with the missing values?

90: How do you change the initial value of SUM variable?

91: How do you consider the value of zero in SAS while using Boolean expressions?

92: While creating a new character variable in the ASSIGNMENT statement, how is the length of the variable determined?

93: Is it possible to assign length to a character variable created using ASSIGNMENT statement?

94: What is the function of KEEP= option?

95: HOW is DROP statement used in SAS procedure?

96: Which form of the DO statement checks the condition before each iteration of DO loop?

97:   What is the result of the following IF statement?

if *setno*=23 or 45;

98:   Suppose you have a Data Set in which the variables are assigned with permanent labels. But, you are submitting a proc step in which you are assigning a new label to one of the variables. What will be displayed as the label for the variable- new one or the one which is permanently stored?

## Combining Data Sets

99:   How do you read a Data Set *questionset1* which is stored in the library *'exam'*?

100:  You might be aware of the DROP= option. What criteria should you use to decide whether to place the option in the SET statement or DATA statement?

101:  Which variables are created automatically when you are using BY statement along with the SET statement?

102:  How do you go straight to an observation in a Data Set without considering preceding observations?

103:  What happens if we specify invalid values for POINT= variables?

104:  How do you detect an end of Data Set while reading data?

105:  Which conditions have to be checked while using POINT= option?

106:  While performing one-to-one reading does the resulting Data Set contain all the observations and variables from the input Data Sets?

107:  What is the maximum number of Data Sets which can be given as an input for APPEND procedure?

108:  How does concatenating combine the input Data Sets?

109:  What is the prerequisite for two Data Sets to be merged by MERGE statement?

110:  How do you use the RENAME Data Set option?

111:  How many variables can be renamed at one time using RENAME= option?

112:  How does one-to-one merging produce output?

113:  What is the functionality of IN= Data Set option?

114: What is the difference between PROC APPEND and concatenate?

115: In which scenarios do you prefer to use the Data Set option KEEP= rather than using the Data Set option DROP=?

## SAS Functions

116: Which function is used to convert character data values to numeric data values?

117: How does SAS store a date value?

118: Explain the significance of the function MDY.

119: What is the significance of DATE function?

120: Which function can be used interchangeably with DATE function?

121: Name some functions which provide results which are analogous to the results produced by any SAS procedure like PROC MEANS.

122: What is a target variable?

123: What happens when a character value is used in arithmetic operations?

124: Is the automatic conversion of character value to numeric and vice versa permissible in WHERE statements?

125: Which function is used to extract the quarter of the year in which a given date is falling?

126: Explain the significance of the function WEEKDAY.

127: Explain INTCK function in detail.

128: Which function is used to extract an integer value from a given numeric value?

129: What happens when you specify an invalid date as an argument in MDY function?

130: Explain INTNX function in detail.

131: What is the functionality of TRIM function?

132: Which function converts all the letters of a character expression to uppercase?

133: Is TRANWRD a character function? Explain the functionality.

134: Which function enables you to search any string within a character variable?

135: Name one function which is used to concatenate the strings in SAS.

136: What is the functionality of SCAN function?

137: Explain the significance of PROPCASE function.

138: What is the output of DAY function in SAS?

139: What is the default length which SCAN function assigns to the target variable?

140: Explain functionality of SUBSTR function.

## DO Loops

141: How do you construct a basic DO loop in SAS or explain the syntax of DO loop.

142: What is the default increment value in DO loop?

143: Can DO loops be used to combine DATA and PROC steps?

144: In SAS is it allowed to decrement DO loop?

145: While specifying the number of iterations in DO loop in SAS, is it possible to list the items in series?

146: Which condition has to be taken care of while specifying variable names to specify the number of iterations in DO loop?

147: How does a DO UNTIL loop execute in SAS?

148: Explain the DO WHILE loop.

149: How do you create observation for every iteration of a DO loop?

150: Is it possible to nest DO loops in SAS?

## Arrays

151: What is the scope of an array in SAS?

152: What will happen if you name an array with a function name?

153: In SAS, is it possible to use array names in DROP, KEEP, LENGTH and FORMAT statements?

154: How do you define a one-dimensional array?

155: How do you indicate the dimension of a one-dimensional array?

156: Which term do you use to specify that the array includes all the numeric variables which are defined in the current data step?

157: Which function is used to determine number of elements in an array?

158: How do you define an array of character variables in SAS?

159: How do you assign initial values to the array element?

160: How do you define a two-dimensional array?

## Raw Data

161: Define nonstandard numeric data.

162: What is free format data?

163: Which features of COLUMN input allow it to be used for reading raw data?

164: Which are the two input styles which SAS uses for reading data in fixed fields?

165: Which parameters are to be mentioned in the input statement while using formatted input?

166: Which numeric INFORMAT can be used if the data contains commas, percentage signs, dashes and dollars?

167: What is fixed length record format?

168: Describe the significance of PAD option.

169: Which parameters are to be mentioned in the input statement while using LIST input?

170: Explain the significance of DLM= option.

171: Is it possible to specify a range of character variables in the input statement, if the values are sequential?

172: What are the main limitations of LIST input?

173: Which option enables you to read the missing values at the end of the record?

174: Which option is specified to read the missing values at the beginning or middle of the record?

175: How does the DSD option affect the way SAS treats delimiters when used with LIST input?

176: What happens when LIST input is used to read character variables whose value has length more than 8?

177: Which modifier is used with LIST input to read the character values having embedded blanks?

178: Which modifier is used along with LIST input to read the

199: Explain double trailing (@@) sign in detail.

200: When is a record which is held by double trailing (@@) line hold specifier released?

201: In which situations is double trailing (@@) not allowed?

202: When is a record which is held by single trailing (@) line hold specifier released?

203: Consider the situation where a record is held by a single trailing (@) sign and another input statement which has an (@) executes?

204: How do you deal with records with varying number of fields while using single trailing sign(@)?

205: Explain STOPOVER option in detail.

206: While reading the data from an external file, which option is used to determine the end of the file condition?

207: Explain FLOWOVER option in detail.

208: Explain TRUNCOVER option in detail.

209: Explain the LINESIZE option.

210: Is it possible to create more than one Data Set in a single data step?

211: How do you rename one or more Data Sets in the same library?

212: How do you modify a label which was permanently assigned in a data step previously?

213: Is it possible to rename variables in a Data Set using Data Sets procedure?

214: Is it possible to copy the Data Sets from one library to another using programming statements?

215: Explain the significance of EXCLUDE statement while using COPY statement.

## HR Interview Questions

1: How would you handle a negative co-worker?

2: What would you do if you witnessed a co-worker surfing the web, reading a book, etc, wasting company time?

3: How do you handle competition among yourself and other employees?

4: When is it okay to socialize with co-workers?

5: Tell me about a time when a major change was made at your last job, and how you handled it.

6: When delegating tasks, how do you choose which tasks go to which team members?

7: Tell me about a time when you had to stand up for something you believed strongly about to co-workers or a supervisor.

8: Tell me about a time when you helped someone finish their work, even though it wasn't "your job."

9: What are the challenges of working on a team? How do you handle this?

10: Do you value diversity in the workplace?

11: How would you handle a situation in which a co-worker was not accepting of someone else's diversity?

12: Are you rewarded more from working on a team, or accomplishing a task on your own?

13: Tell me about a time when you didn't meet a deadline.

14: How do you eliminate distractions while working?

15: Tell me about a time when you worked in a position with a weekly or monthly quota to meet. How often were you successful?

16: Tell me about a time when you met a tough deadline, and how you were able to complete it.

17: How do you stay organized when you have multiple projects on your plate?

18: How much time during your work day do you spend on "auto-pilot?"

19: How do you handle deadlines?

20: Tell me about your personal problem-solving process.

21: What sort of things at work can make you stressed?

22: What do you look like when you are stressed about something? How do you solve it?

23: Can you multi-task?

24: How many hours per week do you work?

25: How many times per day do you check your email?

26: Tell me about a time when you worked additional hours to finish a project.

27: Tell me about a time when your performance exceeded the duties and requirements of your job.

28: What is your driving attitude about work?

29: Do you take work home with you?

30: Describe a typical work day to me.

31: Tell me about a time when you went out of your way at your previous job.

32: Are you open to receiving feedback and criticisms on your job performance, and adjusting as necessary?

33: What inspires you?

34: How do you inspire others?

35: How do you make decisions?

36: What are the most difficult decisions for you to make?

37: When making a tough decision, how do you gather information?

38: Tell me about a decision you made that did not turn out well.

39: Are you able to make decisions quickly?

40: Ten years ago, what were your career goals?

41: Tell me about a weakness you used to have, and how you changed it.

42: Tell me about your goal-setting process.

43: Tell me about a time when you solved a problem by creating actionable steps to follow.

44: Where do you see yourself five years from now?

45: When in a position, do you look for opportunities to promote?

46: On a scale of 1 to 10, how successful has your life been?

72: Tell me about a time when you received feedback on your work and enacted it.

73: Tell me about a time when you received feedback on your work that you did not agree with, or thought was unfair. How did you handle it?

74: What was your favorite job, and why?

75: Tell me about an opportunity that your last position did not allow you to achieve.

76: Tell me about the worst boss you ever had.

# Some of the following titles might also be handy:

1. .NET Interview Questions You'll Most Likely Be Asked
2. 200 Interview Questions You'll Most Likely Be Asked
3. Access VBA Programming Interview Questions You'll Most Likely Be Asked
4. Adobe ColdFusion Interview Questions You'll Most Likely Be Asked
5. Advanced C++ Interview Questions You'll Most Likely Be Asked
6. Advanced Excel Interview Questions You'll Most Likely Be Asked
7. Advanced JAVA Interview Questions You'll Most Likely Be Asked
8. Advanced SAS Interview Questions You'll Most Likely Be Asked
9. AJAX Interview Questions You'll Most Likely Be Asked
10. Algorithms Interview Questions You'll Most Likely Be Asked
11. Android Development Interview Questions You'll Most Likely Be Asked
12. Ant & Maven Interview Questions You'll Most Likely Be Asked
13. Apache Web Server Interview Questions You'll Most Likely Be Asked
14. Artificial Intelligence Interview Questions You'll Most Likely Be Asked
15. ASP.NET Interview Questions You'll Most Likely Be Asked
16. Automated Software Testing Interview Questions You'll Most Likely Be Asked
17. Base SAS Interview Questions You'll Most Likely Be Asked
18. BEA WebLogic Server Interview Questions You'll Most Likely Be Asked
19. C & C++ Interview Questions You'll Most Likely Be Asked
20. C# Interview Questions You'll Most Likely Be Asked
21. CCNA Interview Questions You'll Most Likely Be Asked
22. Cloud Computing Interview Questions You'll Most Likely Be Asked
23. Computer Architecture Interview Questions You'll Most Likely Be Asked
24. Computer Networks Interview Questions You'll Most Likely Be Asked
25. Core JAVA Interview Questions You'll Most Likely Be Asked
26. Data Structures & Algorithms Interview Questions You'll Most Likely Be Asked
27. EJB 3.0 Interview Questions You'll Most Likely Be Asked
28. Entity Framework Interview Questions You'll Most Likely Be Asked
29. Fedora & RHEL Interview Questions You'll Most Likely Be Asked
30. Hadoop BIG DATA Interview Questions You'll Most Likely Be Asked
31. Hibernate, Spring & Struts Interview Questions You'll Most Likely Be Asked
32. HTML, XHTML and CSS Interview Questions You'll Most Likely Be Asked
33. HTML5 Interview Questions You'll Most Likely Be Asked
34. IBM WebSphere Application Server Interview Questions You'll Most Likely Be Asked
35. iOS SDK Interview Questions You'll Most Likely Be Asked
36. Java / J2EE Design Patterns Interview Questions You'll Most Likely Be Asked
37. Java / J2EE Interview Questions You'll Most Likely Be Asked
38. JavaScript Interview Questions You'll Most Likely Be Asked
39. JavaServer Faces Interview Questions You'll Most Likely Be Asked
40. JDBC Interview Questions You'll Most Likely Be Asked
41. jQuery Interview Questions You'll Most Likely Be Asked
42. JSP-Servlet Interview Questions You'll Most Likely Be Asked
43. JUnit Interview Questions You'll Most Likely Be Asked
44. Linux Interview Questions You'll Most Likely Be Asked
45. Linux System Administrator Interview Questions You'll Most Likely Be Asked
46. Mac OS X Lion Interview Questions You'll Most Likely Be Asked
47. Mac OS X Snow Leopard Interview Questions You'll Most Likely Be Asked
48. Microsoft Access Interview Questions You'll Most Likely Be Asked
49. Microsoft Powerpoint Interview Questions You'll Most Likely Be Asked
50. Microsoft Word Interview Questions You'll Most Likely Be Asked

51. MySQL Interview Questions You'll Most Likely Be Asked
52. Networking Interview Questions You'll Most Likely Be Asked
53. OOPS Interview Questions You'll Most Likely Be Asked
54. Operating Systems Interview Questions You'll Most Likely Be Asked
55. Oracle Database Administration Interview Questions You'll Most Likely Be Asked
56. Oracle E-Business Suite Interview Questions You'll Most Likely Be Asked
57. ORACLE PL/SQL Interview Questions You'll Most Likely Be Asked
58. Perl Programming Interview Questions You'll Most Likely Be Asked
59. PHP Interview Questions You'll Most Likely Be Asked
60. Python Interview Questions You'll Most Likely Be Asked
61. RESTful JAVA Web Services Interview Questions You'll Most Likely Be Asked
62. SAP HANA Interview Questions You'll Most Likely Be Asked
63. SAS Programming Guidelines Interview Questions You'll Most Likely Be Asked
64. Selenium Testing Tools Interview Questions You'll Most Likely Be Asked
65. Silverlight Interview Questions You'll Most Likely Be Asked
66. Software Repositories Interview Questions You'll Most Likely Be Asked
67. Software Testing Interview Questions You'll Most Likely Be Asked
68. SQL Server Interview Questions You'll Most Likely Be Asked
69. Tomcat Interview Questions You'll Most Likely Be Asked
70. UML Interview Questions You'll Most Likely Be Asked
71. Unix Interview Questions You'll Most Likely Be Asked
72. UNIX Shell Programming Interview Questions You'll Most Likely Be Asked
73. Windows Server 2008 R2 Interview Questions You'll Most Likely Be Asked
74. XLXP, XSLT, XPATH, XFORMS & XQuery Interview Questions You'll Most Likely Be Asked
75. XML Interview Questions You'll Most Likely Be Asked

## For complete list visit

# www.vibrantpublishers.com